THE PAR

THE ACTOR

TABLE DES MATIÈRES

PREFACE 5

THE PARADOX OF THE ACTOR 18

DIDEROT TODAY 207

PREFACE

It is the nature of a paradox that it should deal with extremes. Diderot's entertaining work is an apt illustration of this truth. Having persuaded himself that sensibility should have no part in an actor's functions, he goes on to prove that it is one of the misfortunes, and even one of the vices, of the human mind. He is almost as angry with it as Sir Peter Teazle is with everything that sounds like a sentiment. 'Sensibility, cripples the intelligence at the very juncture when a man needs all his self-possession.' <u>Sensibility is the 'disposition which accompanies organic weakness.</u>' It 'inclines one to being compassionate, to being horrified, to admiration, to fear, to being upset, to tears, to faintings, to rescues, to flights, to exclamations, to loss of self-control, to being contemptuous, disdainful, to having no clear notion of what is true, good, and fine, to being unjust, to going mad.' A number of illustrations, real or imaginary, drawn ostensibly from his own experience, enable the philosopher to show that whenever he was unequal to an emergency, whenever a repartee was not ready on his tongue, he was the victim of sensibility. On one occasion he did not lose his head, but was able to reproach a man for refusing help to a starving brother; and this he sets down to the habit of cool reflection, and not to the impulse of indignant humanity. In a word, <u>it is impossible, according to Diderot's theory, for sudden feeling of any kind to find just and adequate expression.</u> Even the orator can never be swayed by real emotion, but must produce his finest effects, must move the multitude at his will, by a simulated fervour which is the outcome of care and calculation.

This is a paradox, indeed; but it is no business of mine to vindicate human nature against the philosopher's fantasy. The basis of his speculation is the character of actors, and as he is sufficiently inaccurate in painting this, there is no necessity to follow him through all the variations of his theme. Diderot had the highest opinion of acting as an art. The great actor, he said, was even a more remarkable being than the great poet. Yet the actor was in some respects a worthless creature, without character or even individuality, and wholly lacking in moral sense. The actors of Diderot's day were not only devoid of sensibility on the stage; they had not a particle of sentiment in private life. They were often seen to laugh, never to weep. They were 'isolated, vagabonds, at the command of the great,' and had 'little conduct, no friends, scarce any of those holy and tender ties which associate us in the pains and pleasures of another, who in turn shares our own.' This picture may have had some truth then; nobody will pretend that it is true now. The stage in Diderot's time did not enjoy that social esteem which makes public spirit and private independence. Actors were the hangers-on of the Court; actresses were, into many cases, worse than hangers-on. 'Want of education, poverty, a libertine spirit,' says Diderot, 'made actors slip on the sock or the buskin;' and to the libertine spirit he frankly confesses when speaking of his own early desire to enter the theatrical profession. 'The stage is a resource, never a choice. Never did actor become so from love of virtue, from desire to be useful in the world, or to serve his country or family; never from any of the honourable motives which might incline a right mind, a feeling heart, a sensitive soul, to so fine a profession.'

When such an assumption is essential to a paradox, it is plain that ingenuity and plausibility are at their most audacious climax. For Diderot's position is nothing short of this — that, though wholly destitute of moral qualifies, the accomplished actor must, by sheer force of imitation, absorb into himself for the purposes of his art the moral qualifies he sees in others. This is not with him an affair of feeling, but of argument. He 'must have penetration and no sensibility; the art of mimicking everything, or, which comes to the same thing, the same aptitude for every sort of character and part.' The obvious answer to this is, that an actor's aptitude, however great may be his versatility, must have limits. He cannot, any more than another man, be born without a temperament, and though his talent may be many sided, <u>his natural idiosyncrasy will impel him more strongly in one direction than in another.</u> It was necessary for the purpose of his paradox that Diderot should assume that sensibility must be a wild, ungovernable emotion, absolutely fatal to the nerve of all who are afflicted by it. The one example Diderot gives of a dramatic artist guided by sensibility leaves no doubt of this. Mlle. Dumesnil, he tells us, 'comes on the stage not knowing what she is going to say; half the time she does not know what she is saying: but the has one sublime moment.' Therefore Mlle. Dumesnil was not a great actress. But Talma thought she was. It is of this actress, as well as of Le Kain, Molé, and Monvel, that he says, 'It was only by a faithful imitation of truth and nature that they succeeded in creating those powerful emotions in an enlightened nation which full exist in the recollections of those who heard them.' For an actress to come on the stage not knowing what she is going to say is not the way to give a faithful imitation of truth and nature. 'The extravagant mature who loses her self-control has no hold on us; that is gained by the man who is self-controlled.' But is there no such thing as inspiration? 'Certainly there is,' replies the philosopher. 'You may have your sublime moments, but they must come when the man of genius is hovering between nature and his sketch of it, and keeping a watchful eye on both. Cool reflection must bring the fury of enthusiasm to its bearings.' Exactly; but this is scarcely the bearing of the paradox, for why should not the man of sensibility exercise cool reflection and a watchful eye when the ideas suggested by his emotions are subjected to the test of his judgment? When Macready played Virginius after burying his loved daughter he confessed that his real experience gave a new force to his acting in the most pathetic situations of the play. Are we to suppose that this was a delusion, or that the sensibility of the man was a genuine aid to the actor? Bannister said of John Kemble that he was never pathetic, because he had no children. From this I infer, that Bannister found that the moral quality derived from his domestic associations had much to do with his own acting. And John Bannister was a great actor. Talma says, that when deeply moved he found himself making 'a rapid and fugitive observation on the alteration of his voice, and on a certain spasmodic vibration it contracted in tears.' Has not die actor who can thus make his own feelings part of his art an advantage over the actor who never feels, but makes his observations solely from the sensibility of others? Untrained actors, yielding to excitement on the stage, have been known to stumble against the wings in impassioned exit. But it is quite possible to feel all the excitement of the situation and yet be perfectly self-possessed. This is art which the actor who loses his head has not mastered. It is necessary to this art that the mind should have, as it were, a <u>double consciousness,</u> in which all the emotions proper to the occasion may have full sway, while the actor is all the time on the alert for every detail of his method.

'I call sensibility,' says Talma, 'that faculty of exaltation which agitates an actor, takes possession of his senses, shakes even his very soul, and enables him to enter into the most tragic situations, and the mort terrible of the passions, as if they were his own. The intelligence which accompanies sensibility judges the impressions which the latter has made us feel; it selects, arranges them, and subjects them to calculation. It aids us to direct the employment of our physical and intellectual forces — to judge between the relations which are between the poet and the situation or the character of the personages, and sometimes to add the shades that are wanting, or that language cannot express: to complete, in fine, their expression by action and physiognomy.' That, in a small compass, is the whole matter. It would be impossible to give a more perfect description of the art of acting in a few words. Talma does not assume that die intelligent actor who does not feel cannot be an admirable artist. 'The inspired actor will so associate you with the emotions he feels that he will not leave you the liberty of judgment; the other, by his prudent and irreproachable acting, will leave your faculties at liberty to reason on the matter at your ease.' Nor need it be contended that the actor of sensibility must always feel — that, as Diderot suggests, he must wear himself out by excess of soul. It may be that his playing will be more spirited one night than another. It is possible to see in the writings of the greatest novelists where the pen has flagged, and where the deftness of the workman is more conspicuous than the inspiration of the man of genius. But the actor who combines the electric force of a strong personality with a mastery of the resources of his art, must have a greater power over his audiences than the passionless actor who gives a most artistic simulation of the emotions he never experiences.

It will be observed that Diderot lays great stress upon the divorce between Nature and the Stage. He was thinking of the stage of Racine, and not of the stage of Shakespeare. He quotes Garrick to the effect that 'an actor who will play you a scene of Shakespeare to perfection is ignorant of the first principles of declamation needed by Racine.' Garrick made a revolution in English declamation by showing that Hamlet's advice to the players might be literally obeyed. But to French critics of that day this was rank heresy. They would not admit that it was the function of tragic poets and actors to hold the mirror up to Nature. Diderot points out that people do not speak on the stage as they do in the street. Every jealous man does not utter laments as pathetic and eloquent as Othello's, but these are nonetheless human because they are couched in splendid diction. They move the hearer because they are the utterance of a man's agony. But to Diderot the creations of Racine were out of this sphere of human emotion. They were grand ideal types, which could not express themselves in simple language; they required an artificial declamation, in which anything like a natural tone would have been a sacrilege. So the chances that the sensibility of the actor would be in keeping with the stilted method he was expected to adopt were necessarily few.

If actors feel, how is it, asks our author, that they can quarrel or make love on the stage all the while they are conducting some scene of great pith and moment, by which the audience is deeply moved? Diderot illustrates this difficulty with much wit. It is sufficient to reply, that <u>the experience of the actor is often superior to the perceptions of his audience</u>; and that <u>to feel love or aversion for a character in a play it is not necessary to entertain one sentiment or the other for the actor or actress who represents that character</u>. The whole soul of an actor may be

[margin note: what about the person they are representing?]

engaged in Hamlet's revenge upon Claudius, but he need not on that account feel any desire to slay the excellent gentleman who enacts the king.

Perhaps it will always be an open question how far sensibility and art can be fused in the same mind. Every actor has his secret. He might write volumes of explanation, and the matter would full remain a paradox to many. It is often said that actors should not shed tears, that <u>real tears are bad art</u>. This is not so. If tears be produced at the actor's will and under his control, they are true art; and happy is the actor who numbers them amongst this gifts. The exaltation of sensibility in art may be difficult to define, but it is nonetheless real to all who have felt its power.

THE PARADOX OF THE ACTOR

THE FIRST SPEAKER.

Let us talk no more of that.

THE SECOND SPEAKER.

Why?

THE FIRST.

It is the work of a friend of yours.[1]

---

[1] The work referred to was *Garrick, ou les Acteurs Anglais*, a translation by Antonio Fabio Sticotti of an English pamphlet. The translation appeared in Paris in 1769. Sticotti was one of the *Comédiens du Roi de la Troupe Italienne*, was famous in the parts both of Pierrot and of Pantalon, and was popular in private life. A mort interesting account of the

THE SECOND.

What does that matter?

THE FIRST.

A good deal. What is gained by accepting the alternatives of holding his talent or my judgment cheap, of going back on the good opinion you hold either of him or of

---

Italian company in Paris, and of how by degrees they came to act in French and to play French pieces, will be found in M. Campardon's book, *Les Comédiens du Roi de la Troupe Italienne*, (Paris: Berger-Levrault et Cie.)

I have, with consderable trouble, procured a copy of Sticotti's work in a second edition published, without his name on the title-page, in Paris by 'J. P. Costard, Libraire, Rue Saint Jean-de-Beauvais. M.DCC.LXX.' It is a free version, with many additions, of *The Actor, or a Treatise on the Art of Playing*. (London: Printed for R. Griffiths, at the Dunciad in Pater-noster Row. MDCCLV.)

me?

THE SECOND.

That will not be the result; and were it so it would make no hole in my friendship for both of you, founded as it is on firmer grounds.

THE FIRST.

May be.

THE SECOND.

It is so. Do you know of what you just now remind me? Of an author I know who fell on his knees to a woman he loved to beg her not to go to the first night of a piece of his.

21

THE FIRST.

A modest man, and a prudent.

THE SECOND.

He was afraid that her affection might hang on the amount of his literary fame.

THE FIRST.

Like enough.

THE SECOND.

That a public check might lessen him somewhat in his mistress's eyes.

THE FIRST.

That loss of love would follow on loss of reputation. That strikes you as absurd?

THE SECOND.

It was thought to be so. The box was taken; he had a complete success; and you may guess how he was embraced, made much of, caressed.

THE FIRST.

He would have been made all the more of if the piece had been hissed.

THE SECOND.

I am sure I am right.

THE FIRST.

And I hold to my view.

THE SECOND.

Hold to it by all means; but remember that I at least am not a woman, and that I am anxious you should explain yourself.

THE FIRST.

Absolutely?

THE SECOND.

Absolutely.

THE FIRST.

I should find it much easier to say nothing than to veil what I really think.

THE SECOND.

Of course.

THE FIRST.

I shall be uncompromising.

THE SECOND.

That is just what my friend would like you to be.

THE FIRST.

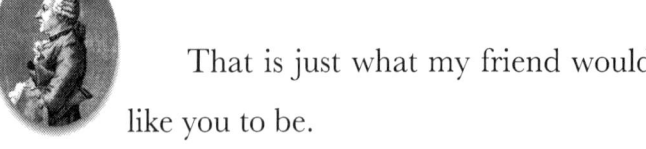

Well then, as I must speak — his work, crabbed, obscure, complicated, bombastic as it is in style, is yet full of commonplace. A great dramatic artist will not be a bit the better, a poor actor not a bit the less inefficient, for reading it. It is Nature who bestows personal gifts — appearance, voice, judgment and tact. It is the study of the great models, the knowledge of the human heart, the habit of society, earnest work, experience, close acquaintance with the boards, which perfect Nature's gifts. <u>The actor who is merely a mimic can count upon being always tolerable; his playing will call neither for praise nor for blame</u>.

THE SECOND.

Or else for nothing but blame.

THE FIRST.

Granted. The actor who goes by Nature alone is often detestable, sometimes excellent. But in whatever line, beware of a level mediocrity. No matter how harshly a beginner is treated, one may easily foretell his future success. It is only the incapables who are stifled by cries of 'Off ! off !'[2] How should Nature without Art make a great actor when nothing happens on the stage exactly as it happens in nature, and when dramatic poems are all

---

[2] Lord Beaconsfield's 'You shall hear me one day,' at the end of his first unsuccessful and derided speech in the House of Commons.

composed alter a fixed system of principles? And how can a part be played in the same way by two different actors when, even with the clearest, the most precise, the most forceful of writers, words are no more, and never can be more, than symbols, indicating a thought, a feeling, or an idea; symbols which need action, gesture, intonation, expression, and a whole context of circumstance, to give them their full significance? When you have heard these words —

'Que sait là votre main?

Je tâte votre habit, l'étoffe en est moelleuse,'

what do you know of their meaning? Nothing. Weigh well what follows, and remember how often and how easily it happens that two speakers may use the same words to express entirely different thoughts and matters. The instance I am going to cite is a very singular one; it is the very work of your friend that we have ben discussing.

Ask a French actor what he thinks of it; he will tell you that every word of it is true. Ask an English actor, and he will swear that, 'By God, there's not a sentence to change ! It is the very gospel of the stage !' However, since there is nothing in common between the way of writing comedy and tragedy in England, and the way of writing stage poems in France; since, according to Garrick himself, an actor who will play you a scene of Shakespeare to perfection is ignorant of the first principles of declamation needed for Racine; since, entwined by Racine's musical lines as if by so many serpents whose folds compress his head, his feet, his hands, his legs, and his arms, he would, in attempting these lines, lose all liberty of action; it follows obviously that the French and the English actors, entirely at one as to the foundness of your author's principles, are yet at variance, and that the technical terms of the stage are so broad and so vague that men of judgment, and of diametrically opposite views, yet send in them the light of conviction. Now hold closer than ever to your maxim, '*Avoid explanation if what you want is a mutual understanding.*'[3]

THE SECOND.

You think that in every work, and especially in this, there are two distinct meanings, both expressed in the same terms, one understood in London, the other in Paris?

THE FIRST.

Yes; and that these terms express so clearly the two meanings that your friend himself has fallen into a trap. In associating

---

[3] This was a favourite aphorism of Grimm, to whom the first sketch of the *Paradoxe* was addressed *à propos of Garrick, ou les Acteurs Anglais*. It is given in vol. viii. of I. Affézat's edition. (Paris: Garnier frères.)

the names of English with those of French actors, applying to both the same precepts, giving to both the same praise and the same reproofs, he has doubtless imagined that what he said of the one set was equally true of the other.

THE SECOND.

According to this, never before was author so wrong-headed.

THE FIRST.

I am sorry to admit that this is so, since he uses the same words to express one thing at the Crossroads of Bussy and another thing at Drury Lane. Of course I may be wrong. But the important point on which your author and I are entirely at variance concerns the qualities above all necessary to a great actor. In my view he must have a deal of judgment. He must have in himself an unmoved and disinterested onlooker. He must have, consequently, penetration and no sensibility; the art of mimicking everything, or, which comes to the same thing, the same aptitude for every sort of character and part.

THE SECOND.

No sensibility?

THE FIRST.

None. I have not yet arranged my ideas logically, and you must let me tell them to you as they come to me, with the same want of order that marks your friend's book. If the actor were full, really full, of feeling, how could he play the same part twice running with the same spirit and success? Full of fire at the first performance, he would be worn out and cold as marble at the third. But take it that he is an attentive mimic and thoughtful disciple of Nature, then the first time he comes on the stage as Augustus, Cinna, Orosmanes, Agamemnon, or Mahomet, faithful copying of himself and the effects he has arrived at, and constantly observing human nature, will so prevail that <u>his acting</u>, far from losing in force, <u>will gather strength with the new observations he will make from time to time</u>. He will increase or moderate his effects, and you will be more and more pleased with him. If he is himself while he is playing, how is he to stop being himself? If he wants to stop being himself, how is he to catch just the point where he is to stay his hand?

What confirms me in this view is the unequal acting of players who <u>play from the heart</u>. From them you must expect no unity. Their playing is

33

alternately strong and feeble, fiery and cold, dull and sublime. Tomorrow they will miss the point they have excelled in today; and to make up for it will excel in some passage where last time they failed.[4] On the other hand, the actor who plays from thought, from study of human nature,' from constant imitation of some ideal type, from imagination, from memory, will be one and the same at all performances, will be always at his best mark; he has considered, combined, learnt and arranged the whole thing in his head; his diction is neither monotonous nor dissonant. His passion has a definite course — it has bursts, and it has reactions; it has a beginning, a middle, and an end. The accents are the same, the positions are the same, the movements are the same; if there is any difference between two performances,

---

[4] This was, according to good authority, the case with Talma in his earlier days; and was certainly so with M. Mounet Sully in his earlier days. Both actors learnt by experience the unwisdom of relying upon inspiration alone.

the latter is generally the better. He will be invariable; a looking-glass, as it were, ready to reflect realities, and to reflect them ever with the same precision, the same strength, and the same truth. Like the poet he will dip forever into the inexhaustible treasure-house of Nature, instead of coming very son to an end his own poor resources.

What acting was ever more perfect than Clairon's?[5] Think over this, study it; and you will find that at the sixth performance of a given part

---

[5] Mlle. Clairon was born in Condé in 1723, and received her first impulse to go on the stage from seeing Mlle. Dangeville taking a dancing lesson in a room of which the windows were opposite to those of the attic in which Clairon's ill-natured mother had locked her up. She made her first appearance with the Italian company at the age of thirteen; then made a great success in comedy parts in the provinces; and at the age of eighteen came back to Paris. Here she appeared first at the Opera; then, in September 1743, at the Français, where she took every one by surprise by choosing to play Phèdre, and playing it with complete success. For twenty years from this time onwards she remained queen of the French stage. She left the stage in 178 and died 1803.

she has every detail of her acting by heart, just as much as every word of her part. Doubtless she has imagined a type, and to conform to this type has been her first thought; doubtless she has chosen for her purpose the highest, the greatest, the most perfect type her imagination could compass. This type, however, which she has borrowed from history, or created as who should create some vast spectre in her own mind, is not herself. Were it indeed bounded by her own dimensions, how paltry, how feeble would be her playing ! When, by dint of hard work, she has got as near as she can to this idea, the thing is done; to preserve the same nearness is a mere mater of memory and practice. If you were with her while she studied her part how many times you would cry out, *That is right !* and how many times she would answer, *You are wrong !*

Just so a friend of Le Quesnoy's[6] once cried, catching him by the arm, 'Stop ! you will make it worse by bettering it — you will spoil the whole thing !' 'What I have done,' replied the artist, panting with exertion, you have seen; what I have got hold of and what I mean to carry out to the very end you cannot see.'

I have no doubt that Clairon goes through just the same struggles as Le Quesnoy in her first attempts at a part; but once the struggle is over, once she has reached the height she has given to her spectre, she has herself well in hand, she repeats her efforts without emotion. As it will happen in dreams, her head touches the clouds, her hands stretch to grasp the horizon on both sides; she is the informing soul of a huge figure, which is her outward casing, and in which her

---

[6] This is a mistake of Diderot's. The person referred to is Duquesnoy the Belgian sculptor.

efforts have enclosed her. As she lies careless and still on a sofa with folded arms and closed eyes she can, following her memory's dream, hear herself, see herself, judge herself, and judge also the effects she will produce. In such a vision she has a double personality; that of the little Clairon and of the great Agrippina.

THE SECOND.

According to you the likest thing to an actor, whether on the boards or at his private studies, is a group of children who play at ghosts in a graveyard at dead of night, armed with a white sheet on the end of a broomstick, and sending forth from its shelter hollow groans to frighten wayfarers.

THE FIRST.

Just so, indeed. Now with Dumesnil[7] it is a different mater: she is not like Clairon. She comes on the stage without knowing what she is going to say; half the time she does not know what she is saying: but she has one sublime moment. And pray, why should the actor be different from poet, the painter, the orator, the musician? It is not in the stress of the first burst that characteristic traits come out; it is in moments of stillness and self-command; in moments entirely unexpected. Who can tell whence these traits have their being? They are a sort of inspiration. They come when the man of genius is hovering between nature and his sketch

---

[7] Mlle. Dumesnil was born in 1713 — not, as M. de Manne says in his *La Troupe de Voltaire*, in 1711. She came to Paris from the provinces in 1737, and made her first appearance at the Français in the same year as Clytemnestra in *Iphigénie en Aulide*. She was admitted the following year, left the stage in 1776, and died in year XI. of the Republic.

of it, and keeping a watchful eye on both. The beauty of inspiration, the chance hits of which his work is full, and of which the sudden appearance startles himself, have an importance, a success, a sureness very different from that belonging to the first sling. Cool reflection must bring the fury of enthusiasm to its bearings.

The extravagant creature who loses his self-control has no hold on us; this is gained by the man who is self-controlled. The great poets, especially the great dramatic poets, keep a keen watch on what is going on, both in the physical and the moral world.

THE SECOND.

The two are the same.

THE FIRST.

They dart on everything which strikes their imagination; they make, as it were, a collection of such things. And from these collections, made all unconsciously, issue the grandest achievements of their work.

Your fiery, extravagant, sensitive fellow, is forever on the boards; he acts the play, but he gets nothing out of it. It is in him that the man of genius finds his model. Great poets, great actors, and, I may add, all great copyists of Nature, in whatever art, beings gifted with fine imagination, with broad judgment, with exquisite tact, a sure touch of taste, are the least sensitive of all creatures. They are too apt for too many things, too busy with observing, considering, and reproducing, to have their inmost hearts affected with any liveliness. To me such an one always has his portfolio spread before him and his pencil in his fingers.

It is we who feel; it is they who watch, study, and give us the result.[8] And then... well, why should I not say it? <u>Sensibility is by no means the distinguishing mark of a great genius</u>. He will have, let us say, an abstract love of justice, but he will not be moved to temper it with mercy. It is the head, not the heart, which works in and for him. Let some unforeseen opportunity arise, the man of sensibility will lose it; he will never be a great king, a great minister, a great commander, a great advocate, a great physician. Fill the front of a theatre with tearful creatures, but I will none of them on the boards. Think of women, again. They are miles beyond us in sensibility; there is no sort of comparison between their passion and ours. But as much as we are below them in action, so much are they below us in imitation. If a man who is really manly drops a tear, it touches us

---

[8] This was so with Goethe, to cake an instance; and not improbably so with Shakespeare.

more nearly than a storm of weeping from a woman. In the great play, the play of the world, the play to which I am constantly recurring, the stage is held by the fiery souls, and the pit is filled with men of genius. The actors are in other words madmen; the spectators, whose business it is to paint their madness, are sages. And it is they who discern with a ready eye the absurdity of the motley crowd, who reproduce it for you, and who make you laugh both at the unhappy models who have bored you to death and at yourself. It is they who watch you, and who give you the mirth-moving picture of the tiresome wretch and of your own anguish in his clutches.[9]

You may prove this to demonstration, and a great actor will decline to acknowledge it; it is his own secret. A middling actor or a novice is sure to

---

[9] Cf. *inter alia* Horace, *Satires*, Book L, Sat. IX.; and *Les Fâcheux*.

contradict you flatly; and of some others it may be said that they believe they feel, just as it has been said of some pious people that they believe they believe; and that without faith in the one case and without sensibility in the other there is no health.

This is all very well, you may reply; but what of these touching and sorrowful accents that are drawn from the very depth of a mother's heart and that shake her whole being? Are these not the result of true feeling? are these not the very inspiration of despair? Most certainly not. The proof is that they are all planned; that they are part of a system of declamation; that, raised or lowered by the twentieth part of a quarter of a tone, they would ring false; that they are in subjection to a law of unity; that, as in harmony, they are arranged in chords and in discords; that laborious study is needed to give them completeness; that they are the elements necessary to the solving of a given problem; that, to hit the right mark once, they have been practised a hundred times; and that, despite all this practice, they are yet found wanting. Look you, before he cries '*Zaïre vous pleurez,*' or '*Vous y ferez ma fille,*' the actor has listened over and over again to his own voice. At the very moment when he touches your heart he is listening to his own voice; his talent depends not, as you think, upon feeling, but upon rendering so exactly the outward signs of feeling, that you fall into the trap. He has rehearsed to himself every note of his passion. He has learnt before a mirror every particle of his despair. He knows exactly when he must produce his handkerchief and shed tears; and you will see him weep at the word, at the syllable, he has chosen, not a second sooner or later. The broken voice, the half-uttered words, the stifled or prolonged notes of agony, the trembling limbs, the faintings, the bursts of fury — all this is pure mimicry, lessons carefully learned, the grimacing of sorrow, the magnificent aping which the actor remembers long after his first study of it, of which he was perfectly conscious when he first put it before the public, and which leaves him, luckily for the poet, the spectator, and himself, a full freedom of mind. Like other gymnastics, it taxes only his bodily strength. He puts off the sock or the buskin; his voice is gone; he is tired; he changes his dress, or he goes to bed; and he feels neither trouble, nor sorrow, nor depression, nor weariness of soul. All these emotions he has given to you. The actor is tired, you are unhappy; he has had exertion without feeling, you feeling without exertion. Were it otherwise the player's lot would be the most wretched on earth: but he is not the person he represents; he plays it, and plays it so well that you think he is the person; the deception is all on your side; he knows well enough that he is not the person.

For diverse modes of feeling arranged in concert to obtain the greatest effect, scored orchestrally, played piano and played forte, harmonised to make an individual effect — all that to me is food for laughter. I hold to my point, and I tell you this: 'Extreme sensibility makes middling actors; middling sensibility makes the ruck of bad actors; in complete absence of sensibility is the possibility a sublime actor.' The player's tears come from his brain, the sensitive being's from his heart; the sensitive being's soul gives unmeasured trouble to his brain; the player's brain gives sometimes a touch of trouble to his soul he weeps as might weep an unbelieving priest preaching of the Passion; as a seducer might weep at the feet of a woman whom he does not love, but on whom he would impose; like a beggar in the street or at the door of a church — a beggar who substitutes insult for vain appeal; or like a courtesan who has no heart, and who abandons herself in your arms.

Have you ever thought on the difference between the tears raised by a tragedy of real life and those raised by a touching narrative? You hear a fine piece of recitation; by little and little your thoughts are involved, your heart is touched, and your tears flow. With the tragedy of real life the thing, the feeling and the effect, are all one; your heart is reached at once, you utter a cry, your head swims, and the tears flow. These tears come of a sudden, the others by degrees. And <u>here is the superiority of a true effect of nature over a well-planned scene</u>. It does at one stroke what the scene leads up to by degrees, but it is far more difficult to reproduce its effect; one incident ill given would shatter it. Accents are more easily mimicked than actions, but actions go straighter to the mark. This is the basis of a canon to which I believe there is no exception. If you would avoid coldness you must complete your effect by action and not by talk.

So, then, have you no objection to make? Ah! I see! You give a recitation in a drawing-room; your feelings are stirred; your voice fails you; you burst into tears. You have, as you say, felt, and felt deeply. Quite so; but had you made up your mind to that? Not at all. Yet you were carried away, you surprised and touched your hearers, you made a great hit. All this is true enough. But now transfer your easy tore, your simple expression, your everyday bearing, to the stage, and, I assure you, you will be paltry and weak. <u>You may cry to your heart's content, and the audience will only laugh. It will be the tragedy outside a booth at fair.</u>[10] Do you suppose that the dialogue of Corneille, of Racine, of Voltaire, or,

---

[10] '*Ce ne fera pas une tragédie, ce fera une parade tragique que vous jouerez.*'

Parade tragique is the brief sketch of a tale of horror given by strolling players outside their booth by way of tempting spectators to the filer performance to be given inside.

let me add, of Shakespeare, can be given with your ordinary voice and with your fireside tone? No; not a bit more than you would tell a fireside story with the openmouthed emphasis fit for the boards.

THE SECOND.

Perhaps Racine and Corneille, great names as they are, did nothing of account.

THE FIRST.

Oh, blasphemy ! Who could dare to say it? Who to endorse it? The merest word Corneille wrote cannot be given in everyday tone.

But, to go back, it must have happened to you a hundred times that at the end of your recitation, in the very midst of the agitation and emotion you have caused in your drawing-room audience, a fresh guest has entered, and wanted to hear you again. You find it impossible, you are weary to the soul. Sensibility, fire, tears, all have left you. <u>Why does not the actor feel the same exhaustion?</u> Because <u>there is a world of difference between the interests excited by a flattering tale and by your fellow-man's misfortune</u>. Are you Cinna? Have you ever been Cleopatra, Merope, Agrippina? Are these same personages on the stage ever historical personages? Not at all. They are the vain images of poetry. No, nor even that. They are the phantoms fashioned from this or that poet's special fantasy. They are well enough on the stage, these hippogriffs, so to call them, with their actions, their bearing, their intonations. They would make but a sorry figure in history; they would raise laughter in society. People would whisper to each other, 'Is this fellow mad? Where in the world does this Don Quixote come from?

Who is the inventor of all this stuff? In what world do people talk like this?'

THE SECOND.

And why are they not intolerable on the stage?

THE FIRST.

Because there is such a thing as stage convention. As old a writer as Æschylus laid this down as a formula — it is a protocol three thousand years old.

THE SECOND.

And will this protocol go on much longer?

THE FIRST.

That I cannot tell you. All I know is that one gets further away from it as one gets nearer to one's own time and country. Find me a situation closer to that of Agamemnon in the first scene of *Iphigenia* than that of *Henri IV*.: when, beset by fears only too well founded, he said to those around him, 'They will kill me; there is nothing surer; they will kill me !' Suppose that great man, that superb and hapless monarch, troubled in the night - watches with this deadly presentiment, got up and knocked at the door of Sully, his minister and friend — is there, think you, a poet foolish enough to make Henri say —

'Oui, c'est Henri, c'est ton roi qui t'éveille;

Viens, reconnais la voix qui frappe ton oreille?'

Or to make Sully reply —

53

'C'est vous-même, seigneur? Quel important besoin

Vous a fait devancer l'aurore de si loin?

A peine un faible jour vous éclaire et me guide,

Vos yeux seuls et les miens sont ouverts...'[11]

THE SECOND.

Perhaps Agamemnon really talked like that.

---

[11] There were believers in poets quite foolish enough for this long after Diderot's time. It was precisely because this sort of diction was dropped for a more natural one in *Hernani* that the play, from its first scene, raised such a storm among the classicists — as he who will may read in the pages of Théophile Gautier. The lines quoted are from the speeches of Agamemnon and Arcas in the opening of Racine's *Iphigénie*, the name Henri being substituted for Agamemnon.

THE FIRST.

No more than Henri IV. did. Homer talks like that; Racine talks like that; poetry talks like that; and this pompous language can only be used by unfamiliar personages, spoken from poetical lips, with a poetical tone. Reflect a little as to what, in the language of the theatre, is being true. Is it showing things as they are in nature? Certainly not. Were it so the true would be the commonplace. What, then, is truth for stage purposes? It is the conforming of action, diction, face, voice, movement, and gesture, to an ideal type invented by the poet, and frequently enhanced by the player. That is the strange part of it. This type not only influences the tone, it alters the actor's very walk and bearing. And hence it is that the player in private and the player on the boards are two personages, so different that one can scarce recognise the player in private. The first time I saw Mlle. Clairon in her own house I exclaimed, by a natural impulse, 'Ah, mademoiselle, I thought you were at least a head taller!'

An unhappy, a really unhappy woman, may weep and fail to touch you; worse than that, some trivial disfigurement in her may incline you to laughter; the accent which is apt to her is to your ears dissonant and vexatious; a movement which is habitual to her makes her grief show ignobly and sulkily to you; almost all the violent passions lend themselves to grimaces which a tasteless artist will copy but too faithfully, and which a great actor will avoid. In the very whirlwind of passion we would have a man preserve his manly dignity. And what is the effect of this heroic effort? To give relief and temperance to sorrow. We would have this heroine fall with a becoming grace, that hero die like a gladiator of old in the midst of the arena to the applause of the circus, with a noble grace, with a fine and picturesque attitude. And who will execute this design of ours? The athlete who is mastered by pain, shattered by his own sensibility, or the athlete who is trained, who has self-control, who, as he breathes his last sigh, remembers the lessons of the gymnasium? Neither gladiator of old nor the great actor dies as people die in their beds; it is for them to show us another sort of death, a death to move us; and the critical spectator will feel that the bare truth, the unadorned fact, would seem despicable and out of harmony with the poetry of the rest.

Not, mark you, that Nature unadorned has not her moments of sublimity; but I fancy that if there is any one sure to give and preserve their sublimity it is the man who can feel it with his passion and his genius, and reproduce it with complete self-possession.

I will not, however, deny that there is a kind of

acquired or factitious sensibility; but if you would like to know what I think about k, I hold it to be nearly as dangerous as natural sensibility. <u>By little and little it leads the actor into mannerism and monotony</u>. It is an element opposed to the variety of a great actor's functions. He must often strip it from him; and it is only a head of iron which can make such a self-abnegation. Besides, it is far better for the ease and success of his study, for the catholicity of his talent and the perfection of his playing, that there should be no need of this strange parting of self from self. Its extreme difficulty, confining each actor to one single line, leads perforce to a numerous company, where every part is ill played; unless, indeed, the natural order of things is reversed, and the pieces are made for the actors. To my thinking the actors, on die contrary, ought to be made for the pieces.[12]

---

[12] Note by the publishers of the small popular edition in

THE SECOND.

But if a crowd of people collected in the street by some catastrophe begin of a sudden, and each in his own way, and without any concert, to exhibit a natural sensibility, they will give you a magnificent show, and display you a thousand types, valuable for sculpture, music, and poetry.

THE FIRST.

True enough. But will this show compare with one which is the result of a pre-arranged plan, with the harmony which

---

Paris: — 'Our modern authors have ended in always writing their pieces for this or that actor. Hence the short life which their productions will have.' The practice, I may add, is, unfortunately, by no means unknown in England.

the artist will put into it when he transfers it from the public way to his stage or canvas? If you say it will, then I shall make you this answer: What is this boasted magic of art if it only consists in spoiling what both nature and chance have done better than art? Do you deny that one can improve on nature? Have you never, by way of praising a woman, said she is as lovely as one of Raphael's Madonnas? Have you never cried, on seeing a fine landscape, 'It's as good as a description in a novel?' Again, you are talking to me of a reality. I am talking to you of an imitation. You are talking to me of a passing moment in Nature. I am talking to you of a work of Art, planned and composed — a work which is built up by degrees, and which lasts. Take now each of these actors; change the scene in the street as you do on the boards, and show me your personages left successively to themselves, two by two or three by three. Leave them to their own swing; make them full masters of their actions; and you will see what a monstrous discord will result. You will get over this by making them rehearse together. Quite so. And then goodbye to their natural sensibility; and so much the better.

A play is like any well-managed association, in which each individual sacrifices himself for the general good and effect. And who will best take die measure of the sacrifice? The enthusiast or the fanatic? Certainly not. In society, the man of judgment; on the stage, the actor whose wits are always about him. Your scene in the street has the same relation to a scene on the stage that a band of savages has to a company of civilised men.

Now is the time to talk to you of the disastrous influence which a middling associate has on a first-rate player. This player's conception is admirable; but he has to give up his ideal type in order to come down to the level of the poor wretch who is playing with him. Then he says farewell to his study and his taste. As happens with talks in the street or at the fireside, the principal speaker lowers his tone to that of his companion. Or if you would like another illustration, take that of whist, where you lose a deal of your own skill if you cannot rely on your partner. More than this, Clairon will tell you, if you ask her, that Le Kain[13] would maliciously make her play badly or inadequately, and that she would avenge herself by getting him hissed. What, then, are two players who mutually support each other? Two personages whose types are, in due proportion, either equal, or else in

---

[13] Le Kain made his first appearance at the Français in September 1750, as Titus in Voltaire's *Brutus*. His success was gained in spite of natural disadvantages in voice and personal appearance. He owed much to Clairon, but more to unceasing study and application. What helped him in the first instance to please critical taste was that, like Garrick, he was the first to venture on varying the conventional sing-song of declamation. Later he and Clairon reformed the stage costume. Much of interest will be found about him in the lately published pamphlet, *Talma on the Actor's Art*. He was great as a tragedian; good as a comedian. He died in February 1778.

them the subordination demanded by the circumstances, as laid down by the poet, is observed. But for this there would be an excess, either of strength or of weakness; and such a want of harmony as this is avoided more frequently by the strong descending to the weak than by its raising the weak to its own level. And pray, do you know the reason of the numberless rehearsals that go on? They are to strike the balance between the different talents of the actors, so as to establish a general unity in the playing. When the vanity of an individual interferes with this balance the result is to injure the effect and to spoil your enjoyment; for it is seldom that the excellence of one actor can atone for the mediocrity, which it brings into relief, of his compagnons. I have known a great actor suffer from his temperament in this way. The stupid public said he was extravagant, instead of discerning that his associate was inadequate.

Come, you are a poet; you have a piece for the stage; and I leave you to choose between actors with the soundest judgments and the coolest heads and actors of sensibility. But before you make up your mind let me ask you one question. What is the time of life for a great actor? The age when one is full of fire, when the blood boils in the veins, when the slightest check troubles one to the soul, when the wit blazes at the veriest spark? I fancy not. The man whom Nature stamps an actor does not reach his top-most height until he has had a long experience, until the fury of the passions is subdued, until the head is cool and the heart under control. The best wine is harsh and crude in its fermenting. It is by long lying in the cask that it grows generous. Cicero, Seneca, and Plutarch, I take to represent the three ages of composition in men. Cicero is often but a blaze of straw, pretty to look at; Seneca fire of vine-branches, hurtful to look at; but when I stir old Plutarch's ashes I come upon the great coals of a fire that gives me a gentle warmth.

Baron, when sixty years old, played the Earl of Essex, Xiphares, Britannicus, and played them well. Gaussin,[14] at fifty, bewitched her audiences in *L'Oracle et la Pupille.*

---

[14] Mlle. Gaussin was the daughter of Antoine Gaussin, Baron's coachman, and Jeanne Pollet, cook to Adrienne Lecouvreur. She made her *début* at the Comédie Française in 1731. She appeared in *Zaïre* and in *Alzire*, but she is best remembered in the part of Inès in *Inès de Castro*, a tragedy by the innovator La Motte, which was much laughed at at the time, though it made even the Regent weep. Mlle. Clairon thus described her sister-comédienne: 'Mlle. Gaussin had the loveliest head, the most touching voice. She had a noble presence, and all her movements had a childish grace which was irresistible; but she was Mlle. Gaussin in everything.' After a brilliant career, on the stage and in the world, this once famous actress, who counted statesmen, poets, and philosophers among her lovers, married an opera-dancer, who ill-treated her, and she died without a friend in 1767.

THE SECOND.

She cannot have looked the part.

THE FIRST.

No; and here you hit perhaps an insurmountable obstacle to getting a perfect stage performance. For that your player must have trod the boards many years, and sometimes a part calls for the blush of youth.[15] If there ever has ben an actress who at seventeen

---

[15] Baron, when eighty years old, came back to the stage to play Rodrigue in the *Cid*. All went well until he had to say, —

> 'Je suis jeune, il est vrai, mais aux âmes bien nées
>
> La valeur n'attend pas le nombre des années.'

The pit laughed once and twice. Baron came to the front and said: 'Gentlemen, I am about to 'begin again a third time; but I warn you, that if any one laughs I shall leave the stage and never come back again.' After this all went well, except that when he knelt to Chimène he could not get up again.

could play Monimia, Dido, Pulcheria, Hermione, why then that is a miracle which will not be repeated.[16] However, an old player does not become ridiculous until his strength has quite left him, or until his fine art will not avail to outweigh the contrast between his real and his supposed age. As on the stage, so is it in the world, where people never fall soul of a woman's conduct unless she has neither talent nor other kind of merit enough to veil her failing.

---

[16] This is an allusion to Mlle. Raucourt's first appearances in 172. She was, as a mater of fact, nineteen at the time. The publishers of the French popular edition have this note on the passage: 'The instance of Rachel has given a triumphant lie to Diderot's assertion.' It may, however, be supposed that the annotators did not mean that Rachel had nothing of her art to learn at seventeen. In our own times, and in England a very distinguished actor was in the habit of saying that no man could possibly play Romeo until he was past fifty, and that then he might perhaps be a little old for the part.

In our days Clairon and Molé[17] played when they first appeared like automata; afterwards they

---

[17] Molé, born in Paris in November 1734, made his first appearance at the Français in 1754. He was an example, like Mrs. Siddons, of a player who triumphed completely over a first failure. Collé wrote of him in his Journal, judging him from his first appearances, that he had a good appearance and nothing more; no passion, art, ease, grace. He was not admitted at first, but he went into the provinces, came back in 1760, and appeared successfully as Andronicus in Campistron's tragedy. From that date his success was assured. He was extremely versatile, and there is a story of him which tells for 'the man with paradox.' Lemercier relates how he was carried away by Molé's acting, and rushed to congratulate him. Molé replied, 'I was not pleased with myself. I let myself go too much; I felt the situation too deeply; I became the personage instead of the actor playing it; I my self-control. I was true to Nature as I might be in private; the perspective of the stage demands something different. The piece is to be played again in a few days; come and see it then.' Lemercier went, and just before the great scene Molé turned to him and said, 'Now I have got my self-control: wait and see.' Never, Lemercier adds, were art and art's effect more striking. Molé died in 1802.

became fine players.[18] Why was this? Did they, think you, acquire more soul, sensibility, heart, in proportion as they grew older?

So to be of age as they are dying? [margin note: So actors have the same...]

It is not long since, after ten years' absence from the stage, Clairon consented to a reappearance. If she played but moderately, was it that she had lost her soul, her sensibility, her heart? Not at all; what she had lost was the memory of her methods. I appeal to the future to confirm me.

THE SECOND.

What ! you believe she will come back to the stage?

---

[18] This was so, as many people well remember, in the case of Signor Mario, who, beginning by being a stick, ended by being so fine an actor that even without his exquisite voice and method of singing he would have been a great artist.

THE FIRST.

Or die of boredom. What substitute is there for the great passions and the house's plaudits?

If such or such an actor or actress were as deeply moved as people suppose, tell me if the one would think of casting an eye round the boxes, the other of smiling to some one at the wing, and, as almost all of them do, speaking straight to the pit; and if the call-boy would have to go to the green-room and interrupt a third player in a hearty sit of laughter by telling him that it's time to go and stab himself?

Come, I will sketch you a scene between an actor and his wife who detested each other; a scene of tender and passionate love; a scene publicly played on the boards, just as I am going to rehearse it, or maybe a trifle better; a scene in which both players surpassed themselves — in which they excited continual bursts of applause from pit and boxes; a scene interrupted half-a-score of times with our clapping hands and exclamations of delight. Their triumph was won in the third scene of the fourth act of Molière's *Le Dépit Amoureux*. The actor plays Eraste, Lucile's lover. The actor's wife plays Lucile, Eraste's adored.

THE ACTOR.

Non, non, ne croyez pas, madame,

Que je revienne encore vous parler de ma flamme.

(THE ACTRESS. *I just advise you.*)

C'en est fait.

(*I hope so.*)

Je me veux guérir et connais bien,

Ce que de votre coeur a possédé le mien.

(*More than you deserved.*)

Un courroux si constant pour l'ombre d'une offense,

(*You end me ! You flatter yourself.*)

M'a trop bien éclairci de votre indifférence :

Et je dois vous montrer que les traits du mépris,

(*Yes, the deepest contempt.*)

Sont sensibles surtout aux généreux esprits

(*Yes, to generous minds.*)

Je l'avouerai, mes yeux observaient dans les vôtres,

Des charmes qu'ils n'ont point trouvés dans tous les autres.

(*Not for want of looking.*)

Et le ravissement où j'étais de mes fers

Les aurait préférés à des sceptres offerts.

(*You have made a better bargain.*)

Je vivais tout en vous;

(*That's not the case; you tell a lie.*)

Et je l'avouerai même

Peut-être qu'après tout j'aurai quoique outragé,

Assez de peine encore à m'en voir dégagé.

(*That would be a bore.*)

Possible que malgré la cure qu'elle essaie

Mon âme saignera longtemps de cette

plaie.

(*Don't be afraid — mortification has set in.*)

Et qu'affranchi d'un joug qui faisait tout mon bien,

Il faudra me résoudre à n'aimer jamais rien.

(*You'll find a way out of that.*)

Mais enfin il n'importe; et puisque votre haine,

Chasse un coeur tant de fois que l'amour vous ramène,

C'est la dernière ici des importunités

Que vous aurez jamais de mes voeux rebutés.

THE ACTRESS.

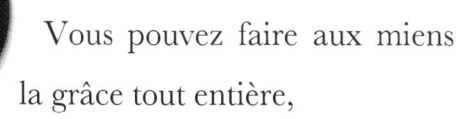

Vous pouvez faire aux miens la grâce tout entière,

Monsieur, et m'épargner encor cette dernière.

(THE Actor. *Sweetheart, you are an insolent baggage, and you shall live to repent this.*)

THE ACTOR.

Eh bien, madame ! eh bien ! ils seront satisfaits,

Je romps avec que vous, et j'y romps pour jamais,

Puisque vous le voulez, que je perde la vie,

Lorsque de vous parler je reprendrai l'envie.

THE ACTRESS.

Tant mieux, c'est m'obliger.

THE ACTOR.

Non, non, n'ayez pas peur.

(THE Actress. Afraid of you? Not I !)

Que je fausse parole ! Eussé-je un faible coeur,

Jusques à n'en pouvoir effacer votre image,

Croyez que vous n'aurez jamais cet avantage

(*Ill-luck, you mean.*)

De me voir revenir.

THE ACTRESS.

Ce serait bien en vain.

(THE ACTOR. *My darling, you are an arrant wretch; but I'll teach you to behave.*)

THE ACTOR.

Moi-même de cent coups je percerais mon sein.

(THE ACTRESS. *I with to Heaven you would !*)

Si j'avais jamais sait cette bassesse insigne.

(*Why not, after so many others?*)

De vous revoir après ce traitement indigne.

THE ACTRESS.

Soit; n'en parlons donc plus.

And so on, and so on. After this double scene — one of love, the other of marriage — as Eraste led his adored Lucile to the wing he squeezed her arm so hard as to tear his sweet wife's flesh, and answered her complaints with the bitterest insults.

THE SECOND.

If I had heard these two simultaneous scenes I don't think I should ever have set foot in a playhouse again.

THE FIRST.

If you think this actor and actress

were moved, let me ask you, was it in the lovers' scene, or the husband and wife's scene, or both? Now listen to another scene between the same actress and another player — her lover. While he is speaking his lines the actress says of her husband, '*He is a brute. He called me... I cannot repeat what he called me.*'

While she, in turn, gives her lines, her lover replies, 'Aren't you accustomed to it by this time?'

And so on from speech to speech. 'Do we sup together tonight?' 'By all means; but how can we escape observation?' 'That you must manage.' 'If he finds out?' 'It will make no odds; and we shall have a quiet evening.' 'Whom shall we ask?' 'Whom you like.' 'The Chevalier, to begin with; he is our mainstay.' 'Talking of him, do you know I could easily get up a jealousy of him?' 'And I could as easily give you cause for it.'

Thus, then, these sensitive creatures seemed to

you to be heart and soul in the speeches spoken out loud, which you heard, while really they were immersed in the speeches spoken under their breath, which you did not hear. You exclaimed to yourself, 'It must be admitted that she is a charming actress; no one listens so well as she does; and she plays with an intelligence, a grace, a conviction, a fine touch, a sensibility, by no means common.' I meanwhile laughed at your exclamations.

Well, this actress plays her husband false with another actor, plays this other actor false with the Chevalier, and plays the Chevalier false with yet another person, with whom the Chevalier catches her. The Chevalier plots a mighty vengeance. He takes his place in the lowest part of the stage-seats[19] (the Comte de Lauraguais had not then rid our stage of this arrangement). Stationed thus he looked forward to disconcerting the faithless wretch by his presence, and by his contemptuous looks to completely upsetting her, and getting her hooted by the pit. The piece begins; the traitress appears; she sees the Chevalier, and without any disturbance to her acting she says 'to him, with a smile, 'Ah ! silly fellow, making a fuss for nothing !' The Chevalier smiles in his turn, and she goes on: 'You are coming tonight?' He makes

---

[19] 'Aux balcons, sur les gradins les plus bas.' The meaning of the phrase may be best explained by the following quotation from Alfred de Musset's essay on Tragedy, written in 1838: — 'How is it that the tragedies of Racine, fine as they are, appear, as it must be confessed they do, cold and formal, like stately statues half vivified? It is because, in 1759, the Count de Lauraguais procured the removal of seats for the audience from the stage, at a cost of thirty thousand francs. Now-a-days Andromache and Monimia stand alone in their vast peristyles, and have an area of sixty feet to walk about in. There are no more marquises to surround the actress and crack a joke with her after every tirade, to pick up Hermione's fan and criticise Theseus's stockings.'

no answer, and she continues: 'Let us make an end of this foolish quarrel; and do you order up your carriage.' And do you know in what scene she put in all this? It was in one of the most touching scenes of La Chaussée,[20] a scene in which the actress was convulsed with sobs and made us drop scalding tears. This startles you; yet it is an exact statement of fact.

THE SECOND.

It's enough to sicken one of the

---

[20] Nivelle de la Chauffée, born in 1692, is looked upon as the founder of drames in France. Schlegel, speaking of Voltaire's *Enfant Prodigue* and *Nanine*, says that 'the affecting drama had been before attempted in France by La Chaussée.' Piron characteristically described La Chaussée's plays as *'Les Homélies du Révérend Père La Chauffée.'* Among his best plays are *Le Préjugé à la Mode* (to which Mlle. Quinault is said to have contributed an act), *Mélanide*, and *La Gouvernante*. La Chaussée died in 1754.

stage.

THE FIRST.

And why, pray? <u>If this kind of people could not achieve such feats, what business would they have on the stage?</u> Now I will tell you a thing I have actually seen.

Garrick[21] will put his head between two folding doors, and in the course of five or six seconds his expression will change successively from wild delight to temperate pleasure, from this to tranquillity, from tranquillity to surprise, from surprise to blank astonishment, from that to sorrow, from sorrow to the air of one overwhelmed, from that fright, from fright to horror, from horror to despair, and thence he will

---

[21] Garrick spent six months in Paris in the winter of 1764-5, when Diderot made his acquaintance.

go up again to the point from which he started. Can his soul have experienced all these feelings, and played this kind of scale in concert with his face? I don't believe it; nor do you. If you ask this famous man, who in himself is as well worth a visit to England as the ruins of Rome are worth a visit to Italy; if you ask him, I say, for the scene of the Pastrycook's Boy he will play it for you; if you asked him directly afterwards for the great scene in Hamlet he would play it for you. He was as ready to cry over the tarts in the gutter as to follow the course of the air-drawn dagger.[22] Can one laugh or cry at will? One shall make a show of doing so as well or ill as one can, and the completeness of the illusion varies as one is or is not Garrick.

I play the fool in this sort sometimes, and with

---

[22] Here is an odd slip on the part of Diderot, who seems to have mixed up Hamlet with Macbeth, and to have left the mistake uncorrected.

success enough to take in men who have knocked about the world a great deal. When I go distracted over the pretended death of my sister in the scene with the Norman lawyer; when in the scene with the First Clerk of the Admiralty I confess to the paternity of the child of a captain's wife; I seem exactly as if I suffered grief and shame: but do I suffer either? Not a bit more now that the thing is in definite stage shape than originally in private company, where I invented these two parts before putting them into a stage play.[23] What, then, is a great actor? A man who,

---

[23] This refers to the *Plan d'un Divertissement Domestique*, to *La Pièce et le Prologue*, and to the final form in which Diderot put the ideas of the rough sketch and the little piece, that final form being die play, *Est-il Bon, est-il Méchant?* The words are a close description of the part of M. Hardouin, in which Diderot sketched his own character. Baudelaire and M. Champfleury tried, many years ago, to get the play acted, the one at the Gaîté, the other at the Théâtre Français. It seems obvious from the text that Diderot, before either *La Pièce et le Prologue* or *Est-il Bon, est-il Méchant?* was written, was in the habit, as many people are now-a-days, of giving little

having learnt the words set down for him by the author, fools you thoroughly, whether in tragedy or comedy.

Sedaine produces the *Philosophe sans le Savoir*. I took more interest in the piece's success than he did; envy of others' talents is not among my vices; I have enough indeed without it. I may call to witness all my brothers in literature, if, whenever they have deigned to consult me as to their work, I have not done all I could to give a fitting answer to this high mark of esteem. The *Philosophe sans le Savoir* trembles in the balance at the first and second performances, and I am very sorry for it; at the third it goes like wildfire, and I am delighted. The next morning I jump into a coach and rush to find Sedaine. It was winter and horribly cold, but I went everywhere where I

---

dramatic sketches in private life, and that he himself played M. Hardouin in *Est-il Bon, est-il Méchant?* in private theatricals.

could hope to find him. I am told he is in the depths of the Faubourg St. Antoine, and my driver takes me there. I rush up to him, I throw my arms round his neck, my voice fails me, and tears run down my cheeks. There you have the man of sensibility, the middling man. Sedaine, reserved and still, looks at me and says, 'Ah ! Monsieur Diderot, you are splendid !' There you have the man of observation — the man genius.

I told this story one day at table in the house of a man whose high talents marked him for the greatest place in the State — in the house of M. Necker.[24] There were many men of letters there; amongst them Marmontel, who is my friend as I am his. He said to me with an ironical air, 'Then, if Voltaire is overcome by the mere narrative of a

---

[24] Necker was not Director-General of Finance till 1777. M. Affézat, the admirable editor of the *Oeuvres complètes de Diderot*, points out that the reference proves that *Le Paradoxe sur le Comédien*, written in 1773, must have been afterwards retouched. It was not published until 1830.

pathetic incident, and Sedaine is undisturbed by the sight of a friend in tears, Voltaire is the ordinary man and Sedaine the man of genius.' This apostrophe put me out, and reduced me to silence, because the man of sensibility, like me, is wrapped up in the objection to his argument, loses his head, and does not find his answer until he is leaving the house. A cold and self-possessed person might have replied to Marmontel, 'Your observation would come better from other lips than yours, for you feel no more than Sedaine, and you too turn out fine work. You, being in the same line with him, might have left it to some one else to be an impartial judge of his talent. But, without preferring Sedaine to Voltaire, or Voltaire to Sedaine, can you tell me what would have come out of the brains of the author of the Philosophe sans le Savoir, of the Déserteur, and of Paris Sauvé, if, instead of passing thirty-five years of his life in damping plaster and cutting stone, he had spent all this time, like Voltaire, like you and me, in reading and thinking on Homer, Virgil, Tasso, Cicero, Demosthenes, and Tacitus? We could never learn to see things as he does; he might have learnt to tell them as we do. I look upon him as one of the latest posterity of Shakespeare; Shakespeare, whom I shall compare neither to the Apollo Belvedere nor to the Gladiator, nor to Antinous, nor to the Farnese Hercules, but rather to the Saint Christopher in Notre Dame — a shapeless Colossus, coarsely sculptured, if you will. Yet we might all walk between his legs and never a head reach to his thighs.'

Now here is another instance of a man reduced at one moment to flat stupidity by sensibility, and the next rising to sublimity by the self-possession following the stifling of his sensibility.

A man of letters, whose name I will hold back,

had fallen into great poverty.[25] He had a wealthy brother, a theologian. I asked the poor brother why the rich one did not help him. 'Because,' he replied, 'he thinks very ill of me.' I obtained his leave to go and fee the theologian. I went, was announced, and told the theologian I had come to talk about his brother. He took me by the hand, made me fit down, and then pointed out that a man of sense takes care to know the client whose case he takes up. Then he said, with some liveliness, 'Do you know my brother?' 'I think so.' 'Do you know his conduct to me?' 'I think so.' 'You do? Then you know…' and herewith my theologian sets off to tell me, with astonishing rapidity and energy, a whole chain of infamies, the one more revolting than the other. My senses feel confused; I am overwhelmed; I lack courage

---

[25] This is the recital of an actual incident. Mme. de Vandeul in her *Memoirs* gives the names and some additional circumstances.

to plead for so vile a wretch as is presented to my view. Luckily the theologian, growing prolix in his philippic, gave me time to recover. By degrees the man of sensibility disappeared, and made way for the man of eloquence; for I may venture to say that on this occasion I was eloquent. 'Sir,' said I coldly to the theologian, 'your brother has done worse than this, and I admire you for concealing the worst of his infamies.' 'I conceal nothing.' 'To all you have told me you might have added that one night, as you left your house to go to matins, he caught you by the throat, and drawing a dagger from beneath his dress was about to plunge it in your bosom.' 'He is quite capable of it; but I have not accused him of it because he never did it.' Then rising suddenly, and fixing a firm, stern look on my theologian, I cried in accents of thunder, and with all the force and emphasis indignation can give, 'And had he done it, would that be a reason for refusing your brother bread?' The theologian, overborne, overwhelmed, confounded, held his peace, walked about the room, came back to me, and granted me an annual allowance for his brother.

Is it at the moment when you have just lost your friend or your adored one that you set to work at a poem on your loss? No ! ill for him who at such a moment takes pleasure in his talent. It is when the storm of sorrow is over, when the extreme of sensibility is dulled, when the event is far behind us, when the soul is calm, that one remembers one's eclipsed happiness, that one is capable of appreciating one's loss, that memory and imagination unite, one to retrace the other to accentuate, the delights of a past time: then it is that one regains self-possession and expression. One writes of one's falling tears, but they do not fall while one is hunting a strong epithet that always escapes one; one writes of one's falling tears, but they do not fall while one is employed in polishing one's verse; or if the tears do flow the pen drops from the hand: one falls to feeling, and one ceases writing.

Again, it is with intense pleasure as with intense pain — both are dumb. A tender-hearted and sensitive man sees again a friend he has missed during a long absence; the friend makes an unexpected reappearance, and the other's heart is touched; he rushes to him, he embraces him, he would speak, but cannot; he stammers and trips over his words; he says he knows not what, he does not hear the answer: if he could see that the delight is not mutual, how hurt he would be ! Judge, this picture being true, how untrue are the stage meetings, where both friends are so full of intelligence and self-control. What could I not say to you of the insipid and eloquent disputes as to who is to die, or rather who is not to die, but that this text, on which I should enlarge for ever, would take us far from our subject? Enough has been said for men of true and fine taste; what I could add would teach nothing to the rest. Now, who is to come to the rescue of these absurdities so common on the stage? The actor and what actor?

<u>The circumstances in which sensibility is as hurtful in society as on the stage are a thousand to one</u>. Take two lovers, both of whom have their declaration to make. Who will come out of it best? Not I, I promise you. I remember that I approached the beloved object with fear and trembling; my heart beat, my ideas grew confused, my voice failed me, I mangled all I said; I cried *yes* for *no*; I made a thousand blunders; I was illimitably inept; I was absurd from top to toe, and the more I saw it, the more absurd I became. Meanwhile, under my very eyes, a gay rival, light-hearted and agreeable, master of himself, pleased with himself, losing no opportunity for the finest flattery, made himself entertaining and agreeable, enjoyed himself; he implored the touch of a hand

which was at once given him, he sometimes caught it without asking leave, he kissed it once and again. I the while, alone in a corner, avoiding a sight which irritated me, stifling my sighs, cracking my singers with grasping my wrists, plunged in melancholy, covered with a cold sweat, I could neither show nor conceal my vexation. People say of love that it robs witty men of their wit, and gives it to those who had none before: in other words, makes some people sensitive and stupid, others cold and adventurous.

<u>The man of sensibility obeys the impulse of Nature, and gives nothing more or less than the cry of his very heart; the moment he moderates or strengthens this cry he is no longer himself, he is an actor.</u>

The great actor watches appearances; the man of sensibility is his model; he thinks over him, and discovers by after-reflection what it will be best to add or cut away. And so from mere argument he goes to action.

At the first performance of *Inès de Castro*, and at the point where the children appear, the pit fell to laughing. Duclos,[26] who was playing Inez, was angered, and cried to the pit: 'Laugh, you blockheads, at the finest point in the piece !' The pit listened, and was silent; the actress went on with her part, and her tears and the spectators' slowed together. Tell me now, Can one pass and repass in this way from one deep feeling to another, from sorrow to anger, from anger to sorrow? I cannot think it; what can very well think is, that Duclos's anger was real, her sorrow pretended.

---

[26] Mlle. Duclos was born in 1670. Her first appearances were made, without much success, on the lyric stage at the Royal Academy of Music in Paris. In October, 1693, she appeared at the Français as Justine in *Geta*, a tragedy by Péchantré. In 1696 she was definitely installed as understudy for Mlle. de Champmeslé in the leading tragic parts. She left the stage in 1733, and died in 1748.

Quinault-Dufresne[27] plays the part of Severus in *Polyeucte*. Sent by the Emperor to harry the Christians, he confides to a friend his real feeling about the calumniated sect. Common sense demanded that this confidence, which might cost him the prince's favour, his honours, his fortune, his liberty, perhaps his life, should be uttered in a low tons. The pit called out, 'Speak louder !' He replied, 'And do you, Sirs, speak less loud !' Had he really been Severus, could he so quickly have again become Quinault? No, I tell you, no. Only the man of self-possession, such as he no doubt

---

[27] Quinault-Dufresne was born in 1693, and made his first appearance at the Français as Orestes in Crébillon's *Electra*, in October 1712. In the month of December following he became an actor of leading parts, both in tragedy and comedy. He left the stage in March 1741, and died in 1759. One of his great parts on the fine was Le Glorieux, and in private life he was in the habit of strutting into the Café Procope and there enlarging upon his genius and his beauty. He married Mlle. Deseine, and it is told of him that after he left the stage he said to his wife, 'I, Quinault-Dufresne, who have conquered the world in the characters of Cæsar and Alexander, my name, alas, is only known to my parrot !'

had, the exceptional actor, the player who is before all a player, can so drop and again assume his mask.

Lekain-Ninias[28] enters his father's tomb, and there cuts his mother's throat; he comes out with blood-stained hands. He is horror-stricken; his limbs tremble, his eyes roll wildly, his hair stands on end. So does yours to see him; terror seizes on you, you are as lost as he is. However, Lekain-Ninias sees a diamond drop which has fallen from an actress's ear, and pushes it towards the wing with his foot. And this actor feels? Impossible. You will not call him a bad actor? Of course not. What, then, is Lekain-Ninias? A cold man, who is without feeling, but who imitates it excellently. It is all very well for him to cry out, 'Where am I?' I answer, 'Where are you? You know well enough. You are on the boards, and you are in the act of

---

[28] That is, of course, Le Kain as Ninias in *Sémiramis*.

kicking a diamond drop off the stage.'

An actor has a passion for an actress; they come together by chance in a stage scene of jealousy. If the actor is poor the scene will be improved; if he is a real player it will lose: <u>in such a case the fine actor becomes himself,</u> and is no longer the grand and ideal type of a jealous man that he has striven for. The proof that if this be so the actor and actress lower themselves to everyday life is, that if they kept to their stilts they would laugh in each other's faces; the bombastic jealousy of tragedy would seem to them a mere clowning of their own.

THE SECOND.

All the same there are truths of Nature.

THE FIRST.

Yes, as in a statue by a sculptor who has given a close transcript of a bad model. You may admire the exactitude, but the whole effect is poor and wretched.

I will go further. A sure way to act in a cramped, mean style, is to play one's own character. You are, let us say, a tartufe, a miser, a misanthrope; you may play your part well enough, but you will not come near what the poet has done. He has created *the* Tartufe, *the* Miser, *the* Misanthrope.

THE SECOND.

And how do you make out the difference between *a* tartufe and *the* Tartufe?

THE FIRST.

Billard, the clerk, is a tartufe; Grizel, the abbé, is a tartufe, but he is not *the* Tartufe. Toinard, the banker, was a miser, but he was not *the* Miser. *The* Miser, *the* Tartufe, were drawn from the Toinards and Grizels in the world; they contain their broadest and most marked features, but there is in them no exact portrait of a given individual; and that is why the real people don't recognise themselves in their types. The comedy that depends on 'go,' even the comedy of character, is an exaggeration. The fun of society is a light froth, which evaporates on the stage; the fun of the stage is an edged tool which would cut deep in society. <u>For imaginary beings we have not the consideration we are bound to have for real beings</u>.

Satire deals with *a* tartufe; comedy *with* the

Tartufe. Satire attacks the vicious; comedy attacks a vice. If there had been only one or two *Précieuses ridicules* in the world they would have afforded matter for a satire, but not for a comedy.

Go to La Grenée,[29] and ask him for a picture of *Painting*; he will think he has done what you want when he has put on his canvas a woman before an easel with her thumb through a palette and a brush in her hand. Ask him for *Philosophy*; he will think he has given it you by producing a woman in careless attire resting her elbow on a desk by lamplight, disheveled and thoughtful, reading or meditating. Ask him for *Poetry*; he will paint the same woman with a laurel-wreath round her brows and a roll of manuscript in her hand. For *Music*, you shall see the same woman with a lyre instead of the roll. Ask him for *Beauty*;

---

[29] A fashionable painter of the time, whose history, curious as it was, need not here be enlarged upon.

ask the fame from a cleverer man than him; and, unless I am much mistaken, he will be persuaded that all you want from his art is a picture of a handsome woman. The same fault is common to your actor and to this painter; and I would say to them, 'Your picture, your acting, are mere portraits of individuals far below the general idea traced by poet and the ideal type of which I hoped to have a representation. This lady of yours is as handsome you like; but she is not Beauty. There is the same difference between your work and your model as between your model and the type.'

THE SECOND.

But, after all, this ideal type may be a phantom!

THE FIRST.

No.

THE SECOND.

But since it is ideal it is not real; and you cannot understand a thing that is impalpable.

THE FIRST.

True. But let us take an art, say sculpture, at its beginning. It copied the first model that came to hand. Then it saw that there were better models, and took them for choice. Then it corrected first their obvious, then their less obvious fault, until by dint of long study it arrived at a figure which was no longer nature.

THE SECOND.

Why, pray?

THE FIRST.

Because the development of a machine so complex as the human body cannot be regular. Go to the Tuileries or the Champs Elysées on a fête-day; look at all the women in the walks, and you will not find one in whom the two corners of the mouth are exactly alike. Titian's Danaë is a portrait; the Love at the foot of the couch is an ideal. In a picture of Raphael's, which went from M. de Thiers' collection to Catherine the Second's, St. Joseph is a common-place man; the Virgin is a real and a beautiful woman; the infant Christ is an ideal. But if you would like to know more as to these speculative principles of art I will send you my *Salons*.

THE SECOND.

I have heard the work praised by a man of fine taste and keen discernment.

THE FIRST.

M. Suard.

THE SECOND.

And by a woman who combines an angel's purity with the finest taste.

THE FIRST.

Madame Necker.

THE SECOND.

Let us go back to our subject.

THE FIRST.

By all means; though I would rather sing the praises of virtue than discuss somewhat idle questions.

THE SECOND.

Quinault-Dufresne, a boaster by nature, played the Boaster [30] splendidly.

---

[30] Le Glorieux.

THE FIRST.

You are right; but how do you know that he was playing his own self? And why should not Nature have made a boaster very near the line between the fine real and the fine ideal, the line on which the different schools find their exercise-ground?

THE SECOND.

I do not understand you.

THE FIRST.

I have explained myself more fully in my *Salons*, in which I commend to your notice the passage on Beauty in general. Meanwhile tell me this: Is Quinault-Dufresne

Orosmanes? No. However, who has taken his place, or ever will take his place, in this part? Was he the man for the *Préjugé à la Mode*? No. Yet with how much truth he played it!

THE SECOND.

According to you the great actor is everything and nothing.

THE FIRST.

Perhaps it is just because he is nothing that he is before all everything. His own special shape never interferes with the shapes he assumes.

Among all those who have practised the fine and valuable profession of actors or lay preachers, one of the most sterling characters, one who showed it the most in his physiognomy, his tone, his bearing, the brother of the *Diable Boiteux* of Gil Blas, of the *Bachelier de Salamanque*, Montmesnil[31]....

THE SECOND.

Son of Le Sage, the father of the illustrious family you have named.

THE FIRST.

... played, with equal success, Aristides in the *Pupille*, Tartufe in the

---

[31] Montménil, son of the celebrated Le Sage, made his first appearance at the Français in May 1726, as Mascarille in *L'Etourdi*. He gained some success, but his fellow-actors counseled him to work in the provinces. This he did, reappearing in Paris in 1728 as Hector in *Le Joueur*. Thenceforward his success was not doubtful. Montménil, Le Mazurier says, played capitally *L'Avocat Patelin*, *Turcaret*, the Valet in *Les Bourgeoises à la Mode*, M. Delorme in *Les Trois Confines*, 'et en général tous les paysans.' He died suddenly in September 1743.

comedy so named, Mascarille in the *Fourberies de Scapin*, the lawyer, or M. Guillaume, in the farce of *Patelin*.

THE SECOND.

I have seen him.

THE FIRST.

And to your astonishment, for all these different parts he had a fitting visage. This did not come by Nature, for Nature had given him but one, his own; the others he drew from Art.

Is there such a thing as artificial sensibility? Consider, sensibility, whether acquired or inborn, is not in place in all characters. What, then, is the quality acquired which makes an actor great in *l'Avare, le Joueur, le Flatteur, le Grondeur, le Médecin malgré lui* (the least sensitive or moral personage yet devised by a poet), *le Bourgeois Gentilhomme, le Malade Imaginaire, le Coeur Imaginaire* — in Nero, in Mithridates, in Atreus, in Phocas, in Sertorius, and in a host of other characters, tragic and comic, where sensibility is diametrically opposed to the spirit of the part? It is the faculty of knowing and imitating all natures. Believe me, we need not multiply causes when one cause accounts for all appearances.

Sometimes the poet feels more deeply than the actor; sometimes, and perhaps oftener, the actor's conception is stronger than the poet's; and there is nothing truer than Voltaire's exclamation, when he heard Clairon in a piece of his, '*Did I really write that?*' Does Clairon know more about it than Voltaire? Anyhow, at that moment the ideal type in the speaking of the part went well beyond the poet's ideal type in the writing of it. But this ideal type was not Clairon. Where, then, lay her talent? In imagining a mighty shape, and in copying it with genius. She imitated the movement, the action, the gesture, the whole embodiment of a being far greater than herself. She had learnt that Æschines, repeating a speech of Demosthenes, could never reproduce 'he roar of the brute.' He said to his disciples, 'If this touches you, or nearly, what would have been the effect *si audivissetis bestiam mugientem?*' The poet had engendered the monster, Clairon made it roar.

It would be a strange abuse of language to give the name of sensibility to this faculty of reproducing all natures, even ferocious natures. Sensibility, according to the only acceptation yet given of the term, is, as it seems to me, that disposition which accompanies organic weakness, which follows on easy affection of the diaphragm, on vivacity of imagination, on delicacy of nerves, which inclines one to being compassionate, to being horrified, to admiration, to fear, to being upset, to tears, to faintings, to rescues, to flights, to exclamations, to loss of self-control, to being contemptuous, disdainful, to having no clear notion of what is true, good, and fine, to being unjust, to going mad. Multiply souls of sensibility, and you will multiply in the fame proportion good and bad actions of every kind, extravagant praise and extravagant blame.

Work, poets, for a nation given to vapours, and sensitive; content yourselves with the tender, harmonious, and touching elegies of Racine; this nation would flee the butcheries of Shakespeare; its feeble spirit cannot stand violent shocks; beware of offering it too vigorous a picture; rehearse to it, if you will,

> 'Le fils tout dégouttant du meurtre de son père,
>
> Et sa tête à la main, demandant son salaire.'

But go no further. If you dared to say with Homer, 'Where you go, unhappy one? You don't know, then, that it is to me Heaven sends the children of ill-fated fathers; you will not receive your mother's last embraces ; even now I see you stretched on the earth; the birds of prey, grouped round your corpse, tear out your eyes, slapping their wings with delight' — If you said this all the women, turning away their heads, would cry, Oh ! horrible !'... And <u>it would be all the worse if this speech, delivered by a great actor, had all the strength of truthful accent.</u>

THE SECOND.

I am tempted to interrupt you to ask what you think of die bowl presented to Gabrielle de Vergy,[32] who saw in it her lover's bleeding heart.

THE FIRST.

I shall answer you that we must be consistent, and if we are revolted at this spectacle neither must we permit Oedipus to show himself with his eyes torn out, while we must drive Philoctetes, tormented by his wound, and expressing his pain with inarticulate cries, off the stage. The ancients had, as I think, an idea of tragedy different from ours; and these ancients — that is the Greeks, that is the Athenians, this fine people, who have left us models in every direction of art unequalled by other nations — Æschylus, I say, Sophocles, Euripides, were not at work for

---

[32] The troubadour story of Gabrielle de Vergy is told, with the lady's name given as Margaret de Roussillon, in chap. xxix. of Scott's *Anne of Geierstein*.

years together to produce the trifling passing impressions which disappear in the gaiety of a supper-party. It was their object to rouse a deep grief for the lot of the ill-fated; it was their object not only to amuse their fellow-citizens but also to make them better. Were they wrong? Were they right? To produce their effect they made the Eumenides rush on the scene, tracking the parricide and guided by the scent of blood in their nostrils. They had too much taste approve the imbroglios, the jugglings with daggers, which are fit only for children. A tragedy is, to my thinking, nothing but a fine page of history divided into a certain number of marked periods. Thus, we are waiting for the sheriff.[33] He arrives.

---

[33] All this talk about *Le Shérif* refers directly to one of Diderot's *scenarios* for plays which he never actually wrote. The *scenario* of *Le Shérif* is published in the eighth volume of M. Affézat's edition of the *Oeuvres complètes de Diderot* (Garnier, Paris). It would, so far as I can see, have made a curiously bad play.

He questions the squire of the village. He proposes apostasy to him. The other refuses. He condemns him to death. He sends him to prison. The daughter implores mercy for her father. The sheriff will Brant it; but on a revolting condition. The squire is put to death. The inhabitants rush on the sheriff. He flies before them. The lover of die squire's daughter strikes him dead with one dagger thrust, and the abominable fanatic dies cursed by all around him. A poet does not need much more material for a great work. Suppose the daughter goes to her mother's tomb to learn her duty to the author of her being; suppose that she is in doubt about the sacrifice of honour demanded from her; that in this doubt she keeps her lover aloof, and will not hear the language of his passion; that she obtains leave to visit her father in prison; that her father wishes to marry her and her lover, and she refuses; that she does sacrifice her honour, and her father is put to death the while; that you are unaware of her fate until her lover, when she is distracted with grief at her father's death, learns what she has done to save him; that then the sheriff comes in hunted by the mob and is struck down by the lover. There you have part of the details of such a work.

THE SECOND.

Part?

THE FIRST.

Yes, part. Will not the young lovers propose flight to the squire? Will not the villagers propose to him to exterminate the sheriff and his satellites? Will there not be a priest who preaches toleration? And in the midst of this terrible day will the lover be idle? And cannot one suppose certain ties between these characters, and make something out of such ties?

Why should not the sheriff have been a suitor of the squire's daughter? Why should he not return with vengeance in his heart against the squire, who has turned him out of the place, and the daughter, who has scorned his suit? What important incidents one can get out of the simplest subject if one has patience to think it over! What colour one can give them if one is eloquent! And you cannot be a dramatic poet without being eloquent. And do you suppose I shan't have a fine stage effect? The sheriff's interrogatory, for instance, will be given with all the pomp of circumstance. No, leave the staging to me, and so an end to this digression.

I take you to witness, Roscius of England, celebrated Garrick; you, who by the unanimous consent of all existing nations art held for the greatest actor they have known ! Now render homage to truth. Have you not told me that, despite your depth of feeling, your action would be weak if, whatever passion or character you had to render, you could not raise yourself by the power of thought to the grandeur of a Homeric shape with which you sought to identify yourself? When I replied that it was not then from yours own type you did play, confess yours answer. Did not avow avoiding this with care, and say that your playing was astounding only because you did constantly exhibit a creature of the imagination which was not yourself?

THE SECOND.

A great actor's soul is formed of the subtle element with which a certain philosopher filled space, an element neither cold nor hot, heavy nor light, which affects no definite shape, and, capable of assuming all, keeps none.

THE FIRST.

A great actor is neither a pianoforte, nor a harp, nor a spinet, nor a violin, nor a violoncello; he has no key peculiar to him; he takes the key and the tone fit for his part of the score, and he can take up any. I put a high value on the talent of a great actor; he is a rare being — as rare as, and perhaps greater than, a poet.

He who in society makes it his object, and unluckily has the skill, to please every one, is nothing, has nothing that belongs to him, nothing to distinguish him, to delight some and weary others. He is always talking, and always talking well; he is an adulator by profession, he is a great courtier, he is a great actor.

THE SECOND.

A great courtier, accustomed since he first drew breath to play the part of a most ingenious puppet,[34] takes every kind of shape at the pull of the string in his master's hands.

THE FIRST.

A great actor is also a most ingenious puppet, and his strings are held by the poet, who at each line indicates the true form he must take.

---

[34] *Pantin.* A figure cut out in card, with strings attached to it. I have used the word puppet to avoid roundabout expression.

THE SECOND.

So then a courtier, an actor, who can take only one form, however beautiful, however attractive it may be, are a couple of wretched pasteboard figures?

THE FIRST.

I have no thought of calumniating a profession I like and esteem — I mean, the actor's. I should be in despair if a misunderstanding of my observations cast a shade of contempt on men of a rare talent and a true usefulness, on the scourges of absurdity and vice, on the most eloquent preachers of honesty and virtue, on the rod which the man of genius wields to chastise knaves and fools. But look around you, and you will see that people of never-failing gaiety have neither great faults nor great merits; that as a rule people who lay themselves out to be agreeable are frivolous people, without any sound principle; and that those who, like certain persons who mix in our society, have no character, excel in playing all.

Has not the actor a father, a mother, a wife, children, brothers, sisters, acquaintances, friends, a mistress? If he were endowed with that exquisite sensibility which people regard as the thing principally needed for his profession, harassed and struck like us with an infinity of troubles in quick succession, which sometimes wither and sometimes tear our hearts, how many days would he have left to devote to our amusement? Mighty few. The Groom of the Chambers would vainly interpose his sovereignty, the actor's state would often make him answer, 'My lord, I cannot laugh today,' or, 'It is over cares other than Agamemnon's that I would weep.' It is not known, however, that the troubles of life, common to actors as to us, and far more opposed to the free exercise of their calling, often interrupt them.

In society, unless they are buffoons, I find them polished, caustic, and cold; proud, light of behaviour, spendthrifts, self-interested; struck rather by our absurdities than touched by our misfortunes; masters of themselves at the spectacle of an untoward incident or the recital of a pathetic story; isolated, vagabonds, at the command of the great; little conduct, no friends, scarce any of those holy and tender ties which associate us in the pains and pleasures of another, who in turn shares our own. I have often seen an actor laugh off the stage; I do not remember to have ever seen one weep. ⌈What do they, then, with this sensibility that they arrogate and that people grant them? Do they leave it on the stage at their exit, to take it up again at their next entrance?⌋

What makes them slip on the sock or the buskin? Want of education, poverty, a libertine spirit. <u>The stage is a resource, never a choice.</u> Never did actor become so from love of virtue, from desire to be useful in the world, or to serve his country or family; never from any of the honourable motives which might incline a right mind, a feeling heart, a sensitive soul, to so fine a profession.

I myself, in my young days, hesitated between the Sorbonne and the stage. In the bitterest depth of winter I used to go and recite aloud parts in Molière and in Corneille in the solitary alleys of the Luxembourg. What was my project? To gain applause? Perhaps. To mix on intimate terms with actresses whom I found charming, and who I knew were not straitlaced? Certainly. I know not what I would not have done to please Gaussin, who was then making her first appearance, and was beauty itself; or Dangevile,[35] who on the stage was so full of charm.

It has been said that actors have no character, because in playing all characters they lose that which Nature gave them, and they become false just as the doctor, the surgeon, and the butcher, become hardened. I fancy that here cause is confounded with effect, and that they are fit to play all characters because they have none.

---

[35] Mlle. Dangeville was born in Paris in 1714. Daughter of a ballet-master and an actress, she made her first appearance at the Français at the age of seven and a half. Her official first appearance was made in 1730, as Lisette in Destouches's *Médisant*. She was admitted two months afterwards, remained on the stage till 1763, and died in 1796. The editor of the *Mémoires Secrets*, echoing public opinion, wrote of her: 'You alone, inimitable Dangeville, never grow old. So fresh, so novel are you, that each time we see you we take to be the first time. Nature has showered her gifts on you, as though Art had refused to endow you; and Art has hastened to enrich you with her perfection as though Nature had granted you nought.' Her first appearances were so successful that it was said of her at the time that she began where great actresses left off.

THE SECOND.

A person does not become cruel because he is an executioner; but an executioner because he is cruel.

THE FIRST.

It is all very well for me to look into these persons' characters; I see nothing in them to distinguish them from their fellow-citizens except a vanity which might be termed insolence, a jealousy which fills their company with trouble and hatred. Perhaps of all associations there is not one where the associates' common interest and that of the public is more constantly and more clearly sacrificed to wretched little pretensions. Envy is worse among them than among authors: this is saying a good deal, but it is true. One poet more easily forgives another the success of a piece than one actress forgives another the applause which marks her out for some illustrious or rich debauchee. <u>You find them great on the stage because, as you say, they have soul; I find them little and mean in society because they have none:</u> with the words and the tone of Camille or the elder Horace they have ever the conduct of Frosine or Sganarelle. Now, to estimate what is at the bottom of their hearts, must I rely on the borrowed reports that are so admirably tricked out, or on the nature of actors and the tenor of their life?

THE SECOND.

But of old Molière, the Quinaults,

Montmesnil, and today Brisart[36] and Caillot,[37] who is equally at home in great and little company, to whose keeping you would fearlessly confide your secrets and your purse, to whom you would trust your wife's honour and your daughter's innocence, with much more security than you would to this or that great gentleman of the Court or this or that venerated priest of our altar…

---

[36] Brizard was born in April 1721, and began his career as an actor by playing in comedy in the provinces. He made his first appearance at the Français in July 1757, as Alphonse in La Motte's tragedy, *Inès de Castro*. He was admitted in the following year, left the stage in 1786, and died in 1791. The *Mémoires Secrets* describe him thus: 'He has the majesty of the king, the sublimity of the pontiff, the tenderness or sternness of the father. He is a very great actor, who combines force with pathos, fire with feeling.'

[37] An account of the great actor Caillot will be found later on in a note on a passage referring to him in greater detail.

THE FIRST.

The praise is not overcharged. What annoys me is, that I do not hear you cite a greater number of actors who deserve or have deserved it. What annoys me is, that among all these possessors *ex-officio* of one quality, which is the valuable and fruitful source of so many others, an actor who is a man of honour, an actress who is a woman of virtue, are such rare phenomena.

Let us conclude from this that it is untrue that they have an exclusive claim to this quality, and that the sensibility which would overcome them in private life as on the stage, if they were endowed with it, is neither the basis of their character nor the cause of their success; that it belongs to them neither more nor less than to any other class of people; and one sees so few great actors because parents do not bring up their children for the stage; because people do not prepare for it by an education begun in youth; and a company of actors is not — as it would have to be among a people who attached the due importance, honour, and recompense to the function of speaking to assembled multitudes who come to be taught, amused, and corrected — a corporation formed like other commonwealths, of persons chosen from every kind of good family, and led to the stage as to the services, the law, or the church, by taste or choice, and with the approval of their natural guardians.

THE SECOND.

The degradation of modern actors is, it seems to me, an unlucky heritage from the old actors.

THE FIRST.

I think so.

THE SECOND.

If plays had been invented in these days, when people have more sensible notions, perhaps... But you are not listening: what are you thinking of?

THE FIRST.

I am following up my first idea, and thinking of the influence plays might have on good taste and morals if players were people of position and their profession an honoured one. Where is the poet would dare propose to men of birth to publicly repeat coarse or stupid speeches? — to women, of character not much lighter than the women we know, to impudently utter before a quantity of listeners such things as they would blush to hear in private at their fireside? If the conditions were altered our playwriters would soon attain to a purity, a delicacy, a grace, that they are further from than perhaps they think. Can you doubt that it would re-act upon the national tone?

THE SECOND.

One might perhaps object that the pieces, old and new, which your well-behaved players would exclude from their repertory, are the very ones we play in private theatricals.

THE FIRST.

And what difference does it make if our fellow-citizens lower themselves to the level of the most wretched players? Would it be the less useful, the less desirable, that our actors should raise themselves to the level of the best citizens?

THE SECOND.

The change s not easy.

THE FIRST.

When I gave the *Père de Famille*, the magistrate of police exhorted me to follow the career.

THE SECOND.

Why did you not?

THE FIRST.

Because, not having achieved the success which I had promised myself with it, and not flattering myself that I could do much better, I grew disgusted with a calling for which I thought I had not enough talent.

THE SECOND.

And why did this piece, which nowadays fills the house before half-past four, and which the players always put up when they want a thousand crowns, have so lukewarm a welcome at first?

THE FIRST.

Some said that our habits were too factitious to suit themselves to a style so simple; too corrupt to taste a style so virtuous.

137

THE SECOND.

That was not without a show of truth.

THE FIRST.

But experience has shown that it was not true, for we have grown no better. Besides, the true, honest has such an ascendency over us, that if a poet's work includes two characters in this kind, and if he has genius, his success will be only the more assured. It is, above all, when all is false that we love the true; it is, above all, when all is corrupt that the stage becomes purest. <u>The citizen who presents himself at the door of a theatre leaves his vices there, and only takes them up again as he goes out.</u> There he is just, impartial, a good friend, a lover of virtue; and I have often seen by my side bad fellows deeply indignant at actions which they would not have failed to commit had they found themselves in the same circumstances in which the poet had placed the personage they abhorred. If I did not succeed at first it was because the style was new to audience and actors; because there was a strong prejudice, still existing, against what people call tearful comedy; because I had a crowd of enemies at court, in town, among magistrates, among Churchmen, among men of letters.

THE SECOND.

And how did you incur so much enmity?

THE FIRST.

Upon my word I don't know, for I have not written satires on great or small, and I have crossed no man on the path of fortune and dignities. It is true that I was one of the people called Philosophers, who were then viewed as dangerous citizens, and on whom the Government let loose two or three wretched subalterns without virtue, without insight, and, what is worse, without talent. But enough of that.

THE SECOND.

To say nothing of the fact that these philosophers had made things more difficult for poets and men of letters in general, it was no longer possible to make one's self distinguished by knowing how to turn out a madrigal or a nasty couplet.

THE FIRST.

That may be. A young rake,

instead of sedulously haunting the studio of the painter, the sculptor, the artist who has adopted him, has wasted the best years of his life, and at twenty he has no resources and talent. What is he to become? A soldier or an actor. You find him, then, enrolled in a country company. He strolls it until he can promise himself an appearance in the capital. An unhappy creature has wallowed in gutter debauchery; tired of the most abject of conditions, that of a low courtesan, she learns a few parts by heart; she goes one morning to Clairon, as the slave of old used to go to the ædile or the prætor. Clairon takes her by the hand, makes her turn round, touches her with her wand, and says to her, 'Go and make the gaping crowd laugh or cry.'

They are excommunicated. The public, which cannot do without them, despises them. They are slaves, constantly dreading the rod of another slave. Think you that the marks of so continual a degradation can fail to have effect, and that under the burden of shame the soul can be strong enough to reach the heights of Corneille?

The despotism that people practise to them they practise in turn to authors, and I know not which is the meaner, the insolent actor or the author who endures him.

THE SECOND.

People like to have their plays acted.

THE FIRST.

On whatever condition. Give your money at the door, and they will weary of your presence and your applause. Well enough off with the small boxes, they have been on the point of deciding either that the author should give up his profits or that his piece should not be accepted.

THE SECOND.

But this project involved nothing less than the extinction of the dramatic author's career.

THE FIRST.

What does that matter to them?

THE SECOND.

You have, I think, but little more to say.

THE FIRST.

You are mistaken. I must now take you by the hand and lead you to the presence of Clairon, that incomparable enchantress.

THE SECOND.

She, at least, was proud of her calling.

THE FIRST.

As will be all who excel in it. The stage is despised by those actors only who have been hissed off the boards. I must show you Clairon in the real transports of anger. If in them she happened to preserve the bearing, the accent, the action of the stage, with all its artifice and emphasis, would you not hold your sides?

could you contain your laughter? What, then, would you tell me? Do you not roundly assert that true sensibility and assumed sensibility are two very different things? <u>You laugh at what you would have admired on the stage;</u> and why, pray? The fact is, that Clairon's real anger resembles simulated anger, and you are able to distinguish between the personality and the passion which that personality assumes. The likeness of passion on the stage is not then its true likeness; it is but extravagant portraiture, caricature on a grand scale, subject to conventional rules. Well, interrogate yourself, ask yourself what artist will confine himself most strictly within the limits of these rules? What kind of actor will most successfully lay hold on this regulated bombast — the man dominated by his own character, or the man born without character, or the man who strips himself of his own to put on another greater, more noble, more fiery, more elevated? One is one's self by nature; one becomes some one else by imitation; the heart one is supposed to have is not the heart one has. What, then, is the true talent? That of knowing well the outward symptoms of the soul we borrow, of addressing ourselves to the sensations of those who hear and see us, of deceiving them by the imitation of these symptoms, by an imitation which aggrandises everything in their imagination, and which becomes the measure of their judgment; for it is impossible otherwise to appreciate that which passes inside us. And after all, what does it matter to us whether they feel or do not feel, so long as we know nothing about it?

He, then, who best knows and best renders, after the best conceived ideal type, these outward signs, is the greatest actor.

THE SECOND.

He, then, who leaves least to the

imagination of the great actor is the greatest poet.

THE FIRST.

I was just going to say so. When by long stage habit one keeps a stage accent in private life, and brings into it Brutus, Cinna, Mithridates, Cornelius, Merope, Pompey, do you know what he does? He couples with a soul small or great, exactly as Nature has cut its measure, the outward signs of an exalted and gigantic soul that is not his own. The result of this is ridicule.

THE SECOND.

What a cruel satire is this, innocent or of malice prepense, on actors and authors!

THE FIRST.

How so?

THE SECOND.

Any one, I imagine, may have a great and strong soul; any one, I imagine, may have the bearing, the manner, the action, appropriate to his soul; and I do not think that the expression of true grandeur can ever be ridiculous.

THE FIRST.

What follows then?

THE SECOND.

Ah, you rogue ! you dare not say it,

and I shall have to incur the general indignation on your behalf. It follows that true tragedy is yet to seek, and that, with all their faults, the ancients came nearer to it than we do.

THE FIRST.

It is true that it delights me to hear Philoctetes say with such simple strength to Neoptolemus, who brings him back the arrows of Hercules, which he stole at Ulysses's instigation, — 'See what a deed you had done! Without knowing it, you had condemned an unhappy wretch to perish of grief and hunger. Your crime is another's, your repentance your own. No; never would you have thought of doing a deed so shameful had you been left to yourself. See then, my child, how important is it for your time of life to keep only honest company. This is what you got by associating with a rascal. And why have aught to do with a man of this character? Would your father have chosen him for your companion and friend? Your good father, who never let any but the first men in the army come near him, what would he say is he saw you with a Ulysses?'

Is there anything in this discourse which you might not address to my son, or I to yours?

THE SECOND.

No.

THE FIRST.

Yet it is finely said.

THE SECOND.

Certainly.

THE FIRST.

And would the tone in which this discourse would be given on the stage differ from the tone in which one would give it in society?

THE SECOND.

I do not think so.

THE FIRST.

And would this tone be ridiculous in private life?

THE SECOND.

Not at all.

THE FIRST.

The stronger the action, the simpler the language, the more I admire it. I am much afraid that for a hundred years on end we have taken the rodomontade of Madrid for the heroism Rome, and mixed up the tone of the Tragic with that of the Epic Muse.

THE SECOND.

Our Alexandrine verse is too harmonious, and is too noble for dialogue.

THE FIRST.

And our verse of ten syllables too futile and too light. However this may be, I would like you never to go to a performance of one of Corneille's Roman pieces, but when you are fresh from reading Cicero's letters to Atticus. How bombastic our dramatic authors seem to me, how repulsive are their declamations, when I recall the simplicity and strength of Regulus's discourse dissuading the Senate and the Roman people from an exchange of prisoners ! Thus he expresses himself in an ode, a poem which includes a good deal more of fire, spirit, and exaltation, than a tragic monologue, — He says:

— 'I have seen our ensigns hanging in the temples of Carthage. I have seen Roman soldiers stripped of their arms, unstained with one drop of blood. I have seen liberty forgotten, citizens with their arms bound behind their backs. I have seen the town gates wide open, and the harvest thick on the fields we ravaged. And you think that, brought back, they will return braver. You add loss to shame. Virtue once driven from a degraded soul never returns. Hope nothing from him who might have died and has let himself be strangled. O Carthage, how great and proud you are in our shame!'

Such was his discourse, such his conduct. He refuses the embraces of his wife and children; he feels himself unworthy of them, like a vile slave. He keeps his eyes moodily fixed on the ground, and scorns the tears of his friends until he has brought the senators to a determination he alone could have proposed, and until he is allowed to go back to his exile.

THE SECOND.

That is simple and splendid, but the really heroic moment was afterwards.

THE FIRST.

You are right.

THE SECOND.

He knew well the torture the savage foe was preparing for him. However, recovering his serenity, he disengages himself from his kinsmen, who seek to put off his return, as easily as in former times he disengaged himself from the crowd of his clients to go and shake off the fatigue of business in his fields at Venafrum or his champaign at Tarentum.

THE FIRST.

Very good. Now lay your hand on your heart and tell me if our poets contain many passages of a tone proper for so grand yet so domestic a virtue, and how from such lips as Regulus's would sound either our tender jeremiades or most of our brave words in Corneille's manner. How many things do I not dare to confide to you ! I should be stoned in the streets were I known to be guilty of such blasphemy; and I am not anxious for any kind of a martyr's crown. If the day comes when a man of genius dare give his characters the simple tone of antique heroism, the actor's art will assume a new difficulty, for declamation will cease to be a kind of sing-song.[38]

For the rest, in saying that sensibility was the mark of a good heart and a middling genius I made no common confession; for <u>if Nature ever moulded a sensitive soul that soul is mine</u>. The man of sensibility is too much at the mercy of his diaphragm to be a great king, a great politician, a great magistrate, a just man, or a close observer, and, consequently, an admirable imitator of Nature — unless, indeed, he can forget himself, distract himself from himself, and, with the aid of a strong imagination, make for himself certain shapes which serve him for types, and on which he keeps his attention fixed, with the aid of a

---

[38] It did, in fact, so cease with Le Kain; at least one gathers as much from all that can be learnt of his method in other authors. This is so much the case that it is at first sight startling to find in one part of Diderot's work a full reference to Le Kain, and in another an implication that no actor had yet ventured to vary the conventional sing-song. But Diderot was as capable of making a slip as Homer.

tenacious memory. Only then it is not his own self that is concerned; it is another's mind and will that master him.

Here I should stop; but you will more readily forgive me the misplacing than the omission of an observation. This phenomenon must surely sometimes have struck you. A budding actor, or let us say a budding actress, asks you to come and see her quietly to form an opinion of her talent. You grant that she has soul, sensibility, and passion. You cover her with praises, and leave her when you depart in hope of the greatest success. But what happens? She appears, she is hissed, and you acknowledge that the hisses are deserved. Why is this? Has she lost her soul, her sensibility, her passion, between the morning and the evening? No; but in her ground-floor room you were both on the same low level; you listened to her regardless of convention; she was face-to-face with you; between you there was no model for purposes of comparison; you were satisfied with her voice, her gesture, her expression, her bearing; all was in proportion to the audience and the space; there was nothing that called for exaltation. On the boards all the conditions were changed: there a different impersonation was needed, since al the surroundings were enlarged.

In private theatricals, in a drawing-room, where the spectator is almost on a level with the actor, the true dramatic impersonation would have struck you as being on an enormous, a gigantic scale, and at the end of the performance you would have said confidentially to a friend, 'She will not succeed; she is too extravagant;' and her success on the stage would have astonished you. Let me repeat it, whether for good or ill, <u>the actor says nothing and does nothing in private life in the same way as on the stage: it is a different world.</u>

But there is a decisive fact, which was told me

159

by an accurate person of an original and attractive turn of mind, the Abbé Galiani, and which I have since heard confirmed by another accurate person, also of an original and attractive turn of mind, the Marquis de Caraccioli, ambassador of Naples at Paris. This is, that at Naples, the native place of both, there is a dramatic poet whose chief care is not given to composing his piece.

THE SECOND.

Yours, the *Père de Famille*, had a great success there.

THE FIRST.

Four representations running were given before the King. This was contrary to court etiquette, which lays down that there shall be as many plays as days of performance. The people were delighted. However, the Neapolitan poet's care is to find in society persons of the age, face, voice, and character fitted to fill his parts. People dare not refuse him, because the Sovereign's amusement is concerned. And when, think you, do the company begin really to act, to understand each other, to advance towards the point of perfection he demands? It is when the actors are worn out with constant rehearsals, are what we call 'used up.' From this moment their progress is surprising; each identifies himself with his part; and it is at the end of this hard work that the performances begin and go on for six months on end, while the Sovereign and his subjects enjoy the highest pleasure that can be obtained from a stage illusion. And <u>can this illusion, as strong, as perfect at the last as at the first performance, be due in your opinion to sensibility</u>? For the rest, the question I am diving into was once before started between a middling man of letters, Rémond de Sainte-Albine,[39] and a great actor, Riccoboni.[40] The man of letters pleaded the cause of sensibility; the actor took up my case. The story is one which has only just come to my knowledge.

I have spoken, you have heard me, and now I ask you what you think of it.

THE SECOND.

I think that that arrogant, decided,

---

[39] Author of *Le Comédien*. 1747.

[40] Riccoboni was bora at Mantua in 1707, and came to France with his parents in 1716. In 1726 he made his first appearance, with success, at the Comédie Italienne, as the lover in Marivaux's *Surprise de l'Amour*. He twice left and twice rejoined the company. In 1749 he made what seemed a third and definitive retreat; but in 1759 he reappeared again as a member of the Troupe Italienne. He died in 1772. Baron Grimm describes him as a cold and pretentious actor. He was the author of various pieces, alone and in collaboration, and published a work called *Pensées sur la Déclamation*.

dry, hard little man, to whom one would attribute a large allowance of contemptuousness if he had only a quarter as much as prodigal Nature has given him of self-sufficiency, would have been a little more reserved in his judgment if you had had the condescension to put your arguments before him and he the patience to listen to you. Unluckily he knows everything, and as a man of universal genius he thinks himself absolved from listening.

THE FIRST.

Well, the public pays him out for it. Do you know Madame Riccoboni?[41]

---

[41] Mme. Riccoboni, wife of the actor at the Comédie Italienne, made her first appearance on that stage in August 1734. She went on acting for forty-six years, and was, according to all accounts, a very clever and interesting woman, and a bad actress. She left the stage in 1760 and died in 1792.

THE SECOND.

Who does not know the author of a great number of charming works, full of intelligence, of purity, of delicacy, and grace?

THE FIRST.

Would you call her a woman of sensibility?

THE SECOND.

She has proved it, not only by her works, but by her conduct. There was an incident in her life which led her to the brink of the tomb. After an interval of twenty years she has not ceased to weep; the source of her tears is not yet dry.

THE FIRST.

Well, this woman, one of the most sensitive that Nature ever made, was one of the worst actresses that ever appeared on the stage. No one talks better on dramatic art; no one plays worse.

THE SECOND.

Let me add that she is aware of it, and that she has never complained of being unjustly hissed.

THE FIRST.

And why with this exquisite sensibility, which, according to you, is the actor's chief requirement, is Mme. Riccoboni so bad?

THE SECOND.

It must be that other requirements fail her to such an extent that the chief one cannot make up for their absence.

THE FIRST.

But she is not ill-looking; she has her wits about her; she has a tolerable bearing; her voice has nothing discordant about it. She possesses all the good qualities that education can give. In society there is no repellent point about her. You see her with no feeling of pain; you listen to her with the greatest pleasure.

THE SECOND.

I don't understand it at all; all I know is, that the public has never been able to make up its quarrel with her, and that for twenty years on end she has been the victim of her calling.

THE FIRST.

And of her sensibility, out of which she could never raise herself; and it is because she has always remained herself that the public has consistently rejected her.

THE SECOND.

Now come, do you not know Caillot?

THE FIRST.

Very well.

THE SECOND.

Have you ever talked with him of this?

THE FIRST.

No.

THE SECOND.

In your place I should be glad to have his opinion.

THE FIRST.

I have it.

THE SECOND.

What is it?

THE FIRST.

Your own and your friend's.

THE SECOND.

There is a tremendous authority against you.

THE FIRST.

I admit it.

THE SECOND.

And how did you know Caillot's opinion?

THE FIRST.

Through a woman full of intellect and keenness, the Princess de Galitzin. Caillot was playing the Deserter,[42] and was still on the spot where he had just gone through the agonies which she, close by, had shared, of an unhappy man resigned to lose his mistress and his life. Caillot draws near the Princess's box, and

---

[42] *Le Déserteur*, a pretty and interesting 'melodrama,' in the old sense of the word, by Sedaine.

with the smile you know on his face makes some lively, well-bred, and courteous remarks. The Princess, astonished, says to him, 'What ! You are not dead? I, who was only a spectator of your anguish, have only just come to myself.' 'No, Madam, I am not dead. My lot would be indeed pitiable if I died so often.' 'Then you feel nothing?' 'Ah, pardon me.' And so they engaged in a discussion which ended as this of ours will end — I she keep to my opinion and you to yours. The Princess could not remember Caillot's arguments, but she had noticed that this great imitator of Nature at the very moment his agony, when he was on the point of being dragged to execution, seeing that the chair on which he would have to lay down the fainting Louise was badly placed, rearranged it as he cried in a moribund voice, *Louise comes not, and my hour is nigh !*[43]

---

[43] Caillot was born in 1733 in Paris, in the Rue St. Honoré, where his father carried on a jeweller's business. In 1743 he

was admitted under the name of Dupuis to the king's private band of musicians. In 1752 he took to acting in the provinces, and in 1760 he made his first appearance with the Troupe Italienne as Colas, in *Favart's Ninette à la Cour.* His success was instant, and increased as his career went on. He was admirable both as a singer and as an actor. Among his greatest successes was Blaise in *Lucile* (Marmontel's words to Grétry's music). In this it was thought unusual daring on his part to appear on the stage in a real peasant's dress, with really dusty boots, and with a really bald head. Grimm wrote of this performance: 'Caillot's playing of the part of Blaise is, I believe, one of the most interesting things that can be seen on any stage. This charming actor puts into his performance so much fineness, so much perfection, that it is impossible to imagine anything better. I defy Garrick, the great Garrick, to play the part better... Caillot in all his parts curies truth in nature and in costume very far. I do not know how he has managed to have just the bald head that Blaise should have.' As a matter of fact, Caillot in Blaise, like Charles Mathews in Affable Hawk, appeared for the first time with his own baldhead uncovered by a wig. Of his presence of mind on the stage there is a story parallel to Diderot's. In *Sylvain* he had to fall at his father's feet and catch him by the knees. The other actor, misunderstanding the movement, drew back, so that Caillot fell face forwards on the stage; but he managed the fall so cleverly that it was taken for a fine stroke of art. He left the stage in 1772, but occasionally returned to fill the place of a sick comrade.

THE SECOND.

I am going to propose a compromise; to keep for the actor's natural sensibility those rare moments in which he forgets himself, in which he no longer sees the play, in which he forgets that he is on a stage, in which he is at Argos, or at Mycenæ, in which he is the very character he plays. He weeps...

THE FIRST.

In proper time?

THE SECOND.

Yes. He exclaims...

THE FIRST.

With proper intonation?

THE SECOND.

Yes. He is tormented, indignant, desperate; he presents to my eyes the real image, and conveys to my ears and heart the true accents of the passion which shakes him, so that he curies me away and I forget myself, and it is no longer Brizart or Le Kain, but Agamemnon or Nero that I hear. All other moments of the part I give up to art. I think it is perhaps then with Nature as with the slave who learns to move freely despite his chairs. The habit of carrying it takes from it its weight and constraint.

THE FIRST.

An actor of sensibility may perhaps have in his part one or two of these impulses of illusion; and the finer their effect the more they will be out of keeping with the rest. But tell me, when this happens does not the play cease to give you pleasure and become a cause of suffering?

[margin note: Is this a bad thing? Do they see it as bad?]

THE SECOND.

Oh, no!

THE FIRST.

And will not this figment of suffering have a more powerful effect than the every-day and real spectacle of a family in tears around the death-bed of a loved father or an adored mother?

[margin note: Why?]

THE SECOND.

Oh, no !

THE FIRST.

Then you and the actor have not so completely forgotten yourselves?

THE SECOND.

You have already pushed me hard, and I doubt not you could push me yet harder; but I think I could shake you if you would let me enlist an ally. It is half-past four; they play *Dido*; let us go and see Mademoiselle Raucourt: she can answer you better than I can.

THE FIRST.

I wish it may be so, but I scarce hope it. Do you think she can do what neither Lecouvreur,[44] nor Duclos, nor Deseine,[45]

---

[44] Mlle. Le Couvreur, born at Fismes (Marne) in 1690, made her first appearance at the Français in May 1717, as Electra in Crébillon's tragedy. She was admitted the same month. She died in 1730, and the fact that she was refused Christian burial in Paris in the same year in which Mrs. Oldfield was buried with all pomp in Westminster Abbey is well known. Le Mazurier, who gives the outlines of the story concerning her on which the play of *Adrienne Lecouvreur* was founded, has also a full and mort interesting account of her acting, from which some brief extracts may here be given. She was of a medium height, with sparkling eyes, fine features, and much distinction of manner. Her voice had naturally few tons, but she had learnt to give them infinite variety. Her diction was extremely natural, and this told greatly in her favour, as all her predecessors, except Floridor and Baron, had adopted a stilted enunciation. She and Baron were said to be the mort loyal members of the company. They both avoided the practice of 'starring' in the provinces, a practice which of lace years has given rise to much disturbance at the Français. The excellence of her acting in scenes where she had to listen instead of speaking was especially remarkable. In all scenes her acting was full of nature and fire. She had every merit that Clairon had, with an amount of feeling that Clairon never possessed. She played many parts in comedy and played them well, but it was as a tragedian that she was unrivalled. Her death was felt as a public misfortune.

nor Balincourt,[46] nor Clairon, nor Dumesnil has accomplished? I dare tell you this, that if our young beginner is still far from perfect, it is because she is too much of a novice to avoid

---

[45] Mlle. Deseine, who afterwards married Quinault-Dufresne, made her first appearance at Fontainebleau before Louis XV. as Hermione in *Andromaque*. Her success was so marked that the king made her a present of a magnificent Roman dress, and she was at once admitted by special ordinance. She appeared as Hermione at the Français in 1725, left the stage in 1732, returned to h in 1733, and quitted it definitely in 1736. She died in 1759. That she was a great actress would be evident, if from nothing else, from the unreserved praise which Clairon bestows on her in her *Memoirs*.

[46] Mlle. Balicourt (so Le Mazurier spells it) made her first appearance at the Français in 1727 as Cléopâtre in *Rodogune*. A month later she was admitted. Her great success was in parts demanding a queenly presence. All that was against her in these was youth, and this Le Mazurier says, with a peculiarly French touch, the pit forgave her with more readiness than it forgave Duclos for remaining on the boards when she was sixty. She left the stage in 1738 and died in 1743.

feeling;[47] and I predict that if she continues to feel, to remain herself, and to prefer the narrow instinct of nature to the limitless study of art, she will never rise to the height of the actresses I have named. <u>She will have fine moments, but she will not be fine</u>. It will be with her as with Gauffin and many others, who all their lives have been mannered, weak, and monotonous, only because they have never got out of the narrow limits which their natural sensibility imposed upon them. You are still bent on marshaling Mademoiselle Raucourt against me?

---

[47] A very distinguished English actor of our own day says of a part in which he has won much well-deserved fame, and which is full of feeling, that his great difficulty was to get over the feeling with which it naturally impressed him. He had to learn the words like a parrot before he could trust himself to give any meaning them. When he first played it he was still a little liable to be carried away by its emotion, and he notes that 'whenever I began really to cry the audience left off crying.'

THE SECOND.

Certainly.

THE FIRST.

As we go I will tell you a thing which has a close enough connexion with the subject of our talk. I knew Pigalle;[48] his house was open to me. One morning I go there; I knock; the artist opens the door with his roughing - chisel in his hand; then stopping me on the threshold of the studio he says, 'Before I let you pass, assure me you will not be alarmed at a

---

[48] Pigalle was born in 1714 and died in 1785. Voltaire called him the French Phidias, and in return Pigalle executed perhaps, the worst statue of Voltaire extant. His *Mercury* gained him his election to the Academy, and led to his visit to Frederick the Great. He presented himself at the Palace at Berlin as *l'auteur du Mercure*, and was told that His Majesty would give him twenty-four hours to leave the kingdom. Frederick's poems had been maltreated in the *Mercure de France*, and he took Pigalle for the critic.

beautiful woman without a rag of clothes on.' I smiled and walked in. He was working at his monument to Marshal Saxe, and a very handsome model was standing to him for the figure of France. But how do you suppose she struck me among the colossal figures around her? She seemed poor, small, mean — a kind of frog; she was overwhelmed by them, and I should have had to take the artist's word for it that the frog was a beautiful woman, if I had not waited for the end of the sitting and seen her on the same level with myself, my back turned to the gigantic figures which reduced her to nothingness. I leave it to you to apply this curious experience to Gaussin, to Riccoboni, to all actresses who have been unable to attain to greatness on the stage.

If by some impossible chance an actress were endowed with a sensibility comparable in degree to that which the most finished art can simulate, the stage offers so many different characters for imitation, one leading part brings in so many opposite situations that this rare and tearful creature, incapable of playing two different parts well, would at best excel in certain passages of one part; she would be the most unequal, the narrowest, the least apt actress you can imagine. If it happened that she attempted a great flight, her predominant sensibility would soon bring her down to mediocrity. She would be less like a strong steed at the gallop than a poor hack taking the bit in its teeth. Then one instant of energy, momentary, sudden, without gradation or preparation, would strike you as an attack of madness.

<u>Sensibility being after all the mate of Sorrow and Weakness,</u> tell me if a gentle, weak, sensitive creature is fit to conceive and express the self-possession of Léontine, the jealous transports of Hermione, the fury of Camilla, the maternal tenderness of Merope, the delirium and remorse

of Phædra, the tyrannical pride of Agrippina, the violence of Clytemnestra? Leave your ever tearful one to one of our elegiac arts, and do not take her out of it.

The fact is, that <u>to have sensibility is one thing, to feel is another</u>. One is a matter of soul, the other of judgment. One may feel strongly and be unable to express it; one may alone, or in private life, at the fireside, give expression, in reading or acting, adequate for a few listeners, and give none of any account on the stage. On the stage, with what we call sensibility, soul, passion, one may give one or two tirades well and miss the rest. To take in the whose extent of a great part, to arrange its light and shade, its forts and feebles; to maintain an equal merit in the quiet and in the violent passages; to have variety both in harmonious detail and in the broad effect; to establish a system of declamation which shall succeed in carrying off every freak of the poet's —

this is matter for a cool head, a profound judgment, an exquisite taste, — a muter for hard work, for long experience, for an uncommon tenacity of memory. The rule, *Qualis ab incepto processerit et sibi constet* [Let the character be kept up to the very end, just as it began, and so be consistent.] rigorous enough for the poet, is fixed down to the minutest point for the actor. He who comes out from the wing without having his whole scheme of acting in his head, his whole part marked out, will all his life play the part of a beginner. Or if endowed with intrepidity, self-sufficiency, and spirit, be relies on his quickness of wit and the habit of his calling, be will bear you down with his fire and the intoxication of his emotions, and you will applaud him as an expert of painting might smile at a free sketch, where all was indicated and nothing marked. This is the kind of prodigy which may be seen sometimes at a fair or at Nicolet's.⁴⁹ Perhaps such people do well to remain as they are — mere roughed-out actors. More study would net give them what they want, and might take from them what they have. Take them for what they are worth, but do not compare them to a finished picture.

THE SECOND.

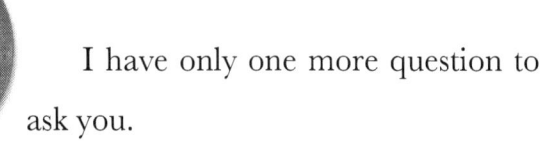

I have only one more question to ask you.

---

⁴⁹ Nicolet was, as may be judged from the context, one of the greatest managers of the *Théâtres de Foire*. He combated desperately, and had not a little to do with upsetting the exclusive rights claimed by the *Comédiens du Roi*, which rights were so skillfully eluded by Piron in his *Arlequin Deucalion*. The whole story, which is given in M. Bonnaffies's *Spectacles Forains* (Paris: Dentu), affords a curious parallel to the similar struggle in England.

THE FIRST.

Ask it.

THE SECOND.

Have you ever seen a whole piece played to perfection?

THE FIRST.

On my word I can't remember it. Stop a bit — yes, sometimes — a middling piece by middling actors.

Our two talkers vent to the playhouse, but as there were no places to be had they turned off to the Tuileries. They walked for some time in silence. They seemed to have forgotten that they were together, and each talked to himself as if he were alone, the one out loud, the other so low that he could not be heard, only at intervals letting out words, isolated but distinct, from which it was easy to guess that he did not hold himself defeated.

The thoughts of the man with the paradox are the only ones of which I can give an account, and here they are, disconnected as they must be when one omits in a soliloquy the intermediate parts which serve to hang it together. He said: Put an actor of sensibility in his place, and see how he will get out of the mess. What did this man do, however? He puts his foot on the balustrade, refastens his garter, and answers the courtier he despises with his head turned on his shoulder; and thus an incident which would have disconcerted any one but this cold and great actor is suddenly adapted to the surroundings and becomes a trait of genius.[50]

[He spoke, I think, of Baron, in the tragedy of the *Comte d'Essex*. He added with a smile:]

Yes; he will tell you she feels when, her head in her confidante's bosom, almost at the point of death, her eyes turned to the third tier of boxes, she suddenly sees an old Justice, who is dissolved in tears, and whose grief expresses itself in ludicrous grimaces, when she exclaims, 'Look up there ! there's a fine face for you !' muttering the words under her breath, like the end of some inarticulate moan. Tel me no such stuff !

If I remember right, this was Gaussin in *Zaïre*.

And this third, whose end was so tragic. I knew

---

[50] The same story of the accidental unfastening of a garter being turned to excellent account by an actor of great presence of mind has in later been referred, probably by confusion with Diderot's story, to the scene in *Ruy Blas*, in which Don Salluste, disguised as a lackey, gives his commands to Ruy Blas disguised as Prime Minister.

him; I knew his father, who asked me sometimes to talk to him through his ear-trumpet.

[Here we are evidently dealing with the excellent Montmesnil.]

He was candour and honour itself. What was there in common between his character and that of Tartufe, which he played so well? Nothing. Where did he find the stiff neck, the strange roll of the eyes, the honeyed tone, and all the other fine touches in the hypocrite's part? Take cane how you answer; I have you.

In a profound imitation of Nature.

In a profound imitation of Nature?

And you will note that the inward signs which chiefly mark the simplicity of the soul are not so much to be seen in Nature as the outward signs of hypocrisy.

You cannot study them there, and an actor of

great talent will find more difficulty in seizing on and examining the one than the other. And if I maintained that of all the qualities of the soul, sensibility is the easiest to counterfeit, since there is scarce a man alive so cruel, so inhuman, that there is no germ of it in his heart, and that he has never felt it — a thing which cannot be safely said of all the other passions, such as avarice, distrust? But an excellent instrument...?

Ah, I understand you. <u>Between him who counterfeits sensibility and him who feels there will always be the difference</u> between an imitation and a reality.

And so much the better; so much the better, I tell you. In the first case the actor has no trouble about separating himself from himself; he will arrive at one blow, at one bound, at the height of his ideal type...

At one blow, at one bound !

You are pettifogging over an expression. I mean that, never being brought back to the little type before him, he will be as great, as astonishing, as perfect an imitator of sensibility as of avarice, hypocrisy, duplicity — of every character that is not his own, of every passion that he does not feel. What the person of natural sensibility shows me will be little; the other's imitation will be strong; or, if the copies should be of equal strength, which I by no means grant you, the one, master of himself, playing entirely by study and judgment, will be, as daily experience shows us, more of a piece than the one who plays part from nature, part from study, part from a type, part from himself. However cleverly the two imitations may be fused together, a keen spectator will discriminate between them even more easily than a great are will discern in a statue the line which marks off either two different styles or a front taken from one model and a back from another... Let a consummate actor leave off playing from his head, let him forget himself, let his heart be involved, let sensibility possess him, let him give himself up to it...

He will intoxicate us.

Perhaps.

He will transport us with admiration.

It is not impossible; but it will be on condition of not breaking through his system of declamation; of not injuring the unity performance; otherwise you will say that he has gone mad. Yes, on this supposition you will, I admit, have a fine moment; but would you rather have a fine moment than a fine part? If that is your choice it is not mime.

Diderot Here the man with the paradox was silent. He walked with long strides, not seeing where he went; he would have knocked up against those who met him right and left if they had not got out of his way. Then, suddenly stopping, and catching his antagonist tight by the arm, he said, with a dogmatic and quiet tone, 'My friend, there are three types — <u>Nature's man, the poet's man, the actor's man</u>. Nature's is less great than the poet's, the poet's less great than the great actor's, which is die mort exalted of all. This last climbs on the shoulders of the one before him and shuts himself up inside a great basket-work figure of which he is the soul. He moves this figure so as to terrify even the poet, who no longer recognises himself; and he terrifies us, as you have very well put it, just as children frighten each other by tucking up their little skirts and putting them over their heads, shaking themselves about, and imitating as best they can the croaking lugubrious accents of the spectre that they counterfeit. Have you not seen engravings of children's sports?[51] Have you not observed an urchin coming forward under a hideous old man's mask, which hides him from head to foot? Behind this mask he laughs at his little companions, who fly in terror before him. This urchin is the true symbol of the actor; his comrades are the symbol of die audience. If the actor has but middling sensibility, and if that is his only merit, will you not call him a middling man? Take care, for this is another trap I am laying for you. And if he is endowed with extreme sensibility what will come of it? — What will come of it? That he will either play no more, or play ludicrously ill; yes, ludicrously; and to prove it you can see the same thing in me when you like. If I have a recital of some pathos to give, a strange trouble arises in my heart and

---

[51] For special instances of such plates M. Affézat refers us to *Les Jeux des Anciens*, by M. Becq de Fouquières (in 8vo. Reinwald, 1869).

head; tongue trips, my voice changes, my ideas wander, my speech hangs fire. I babble; I perceive it; tears course down my cheeks; I am silent. But with this I make an effect — in private life; on the stage I should be hooted.

Why?

Because people come not to see tears, but to hear speeches that draw tears; because this truth of nature is out of tune with the truth of convention. Let me explain myself: I mean that neither the dramatic system, nor the action, nor the poet's speeches, would fit themselves to my stifled, broken, sobbing declamation. You see that it is not allowable to imitate Nature, even at her best, or Truth too closely; there are limits within which we must restrict ourselves.

And who has laid down those limits?

Good sense, which will not play off one talent at the expense of another. The actor must sometimes sacrifice himself to the poet.

But if the poet's composition lent itself to that style?

Then you would have a sort of tragedy very different to what you have here.

And where would be the harm?

I do not know what you would gain, but I know very well what you would lose.

Here the man with the paradox came near his antagonist for the second or third time, and said to him, —

The saying is gross, but it is amusing, and it was said by an actress as to whose talent there are no two opinions. It is a pendant to the speech and situation of Gaussin: she, too, has her head on the breast of Pillot — Pollux; she is dying, at least I think so, and she says to him in a low tone, 'Ah,

Pillot, que tu pues !'

This was Arnould playing Télaïre. At this moment was Arnould really Télaïre? No; she was Arnould, consistently Arnould.[52] You will never bring me to praise the intermediate degrees of a quality which, if it were carried to its fullest extent, and the actor were mastered by it, would spoil all. But let me suppose that the poet has written a scene to be declaimed on the stage as I should recite it in private life, who would play such a scene? No one: no, no one; not even an actor most completely master of his actions; for once

---

[52] Sophie Arnould, the most famous singer of her day, was born in 1740 and died in 1802. She first attracted notice by singing, when little more than a child, before Mme. de Pompadour, and she made her first appearance at the Opera at the age of seventeen. Mlle. Fel taught her singing, Clairon taught her acting. For details concerning her romantic history readers may be referred to MM. de Goucourt's compilation, *Sophie Arnould d'après sa correspondance* (Paris, Dentu). The scene related by Diderot took place in the opera of *Castor et Pollux*.

that he came well out of it he would miss it a thousand times. Success, then, hangs on so little ! This last argument strikes you as not very cogent? So be it, but not the less shall I deduct from it a little bursting of some bubbles, a lowering of some stilts by a few notches, and the leaving things pretty much as they are. For one poet of genius who attained this prodigious truth to nature there would be a vast number of flat and insipid imitators. It is not allowable, under pain of becoming insipid, awkward, and detestable, to go one line below the simplicity of Nature. Don't you think so?

THE SECOND.

I don't think anything. I did not hear what you said.

THE FIRST.

What? We have not been continuing our dispute?

THE SECOND.

No.

THE FIRST.

Then what the deuce were you doing? And of what were you dreaming?

THE SECOND.

That an English actor, called, I think, Macklin (I was at the playhouse that day), having to make his excuses to the pit for his temerity in playing I know not what part in Shakespeare's *Macbeth* after Garrick, said, amongst other things, that the impressions which subjugated actors and submitted them to the poet's genius and inspiration were very hurtful to them. I do not remember the reasons he gave for it, but they were very good, and they were felt and applauded. For the rest, if you are curious about it you will find them in a letter inserted in the *St. James's Chronicle*, over the signature of 'Quintilian.'[53]

---

[53] On this remarkable passage the usually irrefragable M. Affézat has a note which is perhaps equally remarkable, and of which I append a translation. The Italics are my own. 'The fact here recorded is another assistance to fixing approximately the date of Diderot's work. The quarrel between Macklin and Garrick lasted several years, but it was not till 1773 that Macklin took up Garrick's parts, notably that of Macbeth. As he had formerly been the moving spirit of a cabal against Garrick, which, despite his talent, went the length of rotten apples and bad eggs, so now, it is said, Garrick fostered a cabal against Macklin. Less lucky than his compeer, *or, unlike him, being unprovided with a sufficing gang of bruisers*, Macklin had to give up the boards. It was before he

THE FIRST.

So, then, I have been talking all alone all this long time?

THE SECOND.

Very likely — just as long as I have been dreaming all alone. You know that of old actors played women's parts?

---

played Macbeth for the first time that he made a speech, in accordance with English stage custom, bespeaking the indulgence of the audience.'

Diderot has made a hopeless confusion between Garrick's quarrel with Macklin (as to which Macklin published a pamphlet in 1743) and the riotous proceedings which took place on Macklin's third performance of Macbeth at Covent Garden in 1773. These were due to Coleman's simultaneous engagement of William Smith and Macklin, both of whom claimed an exclusive right to acting certain characters, Macbeth amongst them. Full particulars will be found in Kirkman's *Life of Macklin*.

THE FIRST.

I know it.

THE SECOND.

Aulus Gellius recounts in his *Attic Nights* that a certain Paulus, robed in the lugubrious trappings of Electra, instead of presenting himself on the stage with the urn of Orestes, appeared holding in his arms the urn containing the ashes of his own son whom he had just lost; and then it was no vain representation, no petty sorrow of the stage: but the house rang with real shrieks and groans.

THE FIRST.

And you believe that Paulus at this

moment spoke on the stage as he would have spoken at his fireside? No, no. This prodigious effect, as to which I entertain no doubt, depended neither on Euripides's verse nor on the declamation of the actor, but on the spectacle of a desolate father who bathed with his tears the urn holding his own son's ashes. This Paulus was perhaps only a middling actor; no better than that Æsopus of whom Plutarch reports, that, 'playing one day to a full house the part of Atreus, deliberating with himself how he shall avenge himself on his brother Thyestes, there was one of the servants who wished to run suddenly past him, and he (Æsopus) being beside himself with the vehement emotion and the ardour he threw into representing to the life the furious passion of King Atreus, gave him such a blow on the head with the sceptre he held in his hand that he killed him on the spot.' He was a madman, and the tribune ought to have sent him straight off to the Tarpeian rock.

THE SECOND.

Probably he did.

THE FIRST.

I doubt it. The Romans attached so much importance to the life of a great actor, and so little to the life of slave.

But they say an actor is all die better for being excited, for being angry. I deny it. He is best when he imitates anger. <u>Actors impress the public not when they are furious, but when they play fury well.</u> In tribunals, in assemblies, everywhere where a man wishes to make himself master of others' minds, he feigns now anger, now fear, now pity, now love, to bring others into these divers states of feeling. What passion itself fails to do, passion well imitated accomplishes.

Do not people talk in society of a man being a great actor? They do not mean by that that he feels, but that he excels in simulating, though he feels nothing — a part much more difficult than that of the actor; for the man of the world has to find dialogue besides, and to fulfil two functions, the poet's and the actor's. The poet on the stage may be more clever than the actor of private life, but is it to be believed that an actor on the stage can be deeper, cleverer in feigning joy, sadness, sensibility, admiration, hate, tenderness, than an old courtier?

But it is late. Let us go sup.

DIDEROT TODAY

The visitor to the Louvre always remembers the French gallery of the eighteenth century. It is not easy to forget this collection, with its subdued yet splendid color, balance, and harmony of line. Taste — that is the only word which characterizes it; — a taste so pervasive that today it seems rather artificial. Yet the collection has quality, and it has charm; an afterglow of the late renaissance bathes these allegories, these genre-pieces and portraits, and the most casual observer feels the suavity of this eighteenth-century art.

All these relics of that age are so congruous ! Everything combines to produce an impression of harmony. Match the dissonant variety of a modern gallery against this singleness of effect. Here was an age, evidently, that still possessed organized ideals, that still had solidarity. This was a society untroubled by the throes of modern individualism; and we are not surprised to find that, to these people, our beloved word 'original' meant 'eccentric.' Here was an age ruled by the graces, by the social instinct, by the desire to be like one's neighbor. To be like one's neighbor — isn't the ideal manifest in the very portraits about us? Why, they might be all of one family, with their smooth, unruffled faces and their smiling eyes, kinfolk in their affable poise. Spiritually, they are all of one family, and looking them over one by one, you are surprised to discover, on the south wall, a face which startles by its individuality.

It is a painting by Vanloo. A portrait of a writer, with disordered hair and careless dress —

a portrait intime, guiltless of wig and powder. A strong, roughly-cut face, devoid of caste, sensuous but intellectual too, and full of enthusiasm and force. The man looks straight at you, with uplifted head and pen poised, his eyes aflame with inspiration. Is he a poet, or a prophet overcome by a sudden glimpse of the future? Or is he merely a brilliant talker, an improviser, turning from his work to a chance visitor, no more able to resist the temptation to talk than a drunkard the temptation to drink? Who is this man? He is a personality in an age of powder: he is Denis Diderot.

Against the delicate artificial background of the eighteenth century, Diderot stands out in all the vulgar force of democracy. Born in the working classes, without a patron until Catherine of Russia befriends him in his old age, supporting himself and his family by his writings, he typifies the incursion of the Third Estate into literature.

Nay more, Diderot is not merely a journeyman of the pen, he is a literary Bohemian; a skeptic, he will manufacture sermons until he finds scope for real self-expression.

To be sure he was educated by the Jesuits: "in the Temple were forged the hammers which were to destroy the Temple." But neither his education nor his choice of the profession of letters will ever make him an aristocrat like Voltaire. To the end Diderot will remain a plebeian, vulgarly eager and enthusiastic, omnivorous in all his appetites, glutting himself with books and talk as he did with food and drink. Ignorant of measure or poise, devoid of taste or distinction, he is like a force of nature. He is one of those forces which are to destroy the Age of Taste in 1793.

Comte called Diderot "the greatest genius of the eighteenth century." Rousseau could only compare him to Plato and Aristotle. To many-sidedness, to an encyclopedic range of interest,

Diderot added the first idea of modern scientific method: he foreshadowed the revolution of the sciences against the humanities. He had singular insight; more original than Voltaire, he is more radical than the arch-radical Rousseau. It is probable, moreover, that he inspired Rousseau's naturalism, gave him the idea which Jean Jacques seized upon at Vincennes and made the basis of his philosophy, — the notion that nature does all things well. For he furnished his contemporaries with ideas, from Grimm to Galiani; and it was he, not the timid Jean Jacques, who gave the fullest exposition of the doctrine of naturalism by carrying the theory into morality. Most daring of the eighteenth-century thinkers, spending his life in the service of his curiosity, studying all things, interrelating all things, Diderot becomes a seer by his universality no less than by his intuitive vision: he has been claimed as a precursor of positivism, of the theory of evolution, of romantic subjectivity, of the critical 'appreciation,' of realism and naturalism in the novel, of Parnassian poetics, of modern art criticism, of the tendenz-roman and of contemporary social drama. Born two centuries ago, he overwhelms one by his modernity.

And yet he left behind no great book. Attempting every literary genre, even creating new genres, he left no masterpiece, unless it be *Le Neveu de Rameau.* If he gives us a splendid fragment, it is a product of irreflective inspiration — a pure chance. Art, arrangement and selection, is the last thing to ask of him; he seeks nothing but self-expression. Writing as the ideas come to him, never polishing or correcting, he was content to circulate his finest pages in manuscript, satisfied if they pleased his correspondents or his friends. He laughed at the idea of collecting his writings — that mass of material which posterity has gathered into twenty great octavos. Caring nothing for his works and everything for his work, he is, even more than Voltaire, the perfect type of the journalist in literature. But he is a journalist of genius.

It was as a journalist, a leader of thought, a popularizer, that he sank the best of his labors in the Encyclopedia. That is his monument, a huge quasi-anonymous memorial, although his contributions have since been sorted from the rest. A pure publisher's speculation at the outset, a scheme to translate into French the English work of Ephraim Chambers, the enterprise was transformed by Diderot into a veritable means of propaganda. Starting from the idea of Bayle's Dictionary, inspired perhaps by Bacon's *Instauratio*, he magnified the original conception, and the projected work became "a book containing all other books," a synopsis of the efforts of the human mind in its long historical struggle for truth against tradition. He made it, with this, a dictionary of mechanical arts and trades, a sort of prospectus of modern industrialism, and in the absence of trained specialists, spent days in the factories and workshops, learning the processes in order to describe them. He directed the preparation of the plates — some 3,000 in all — which display the trades and manufactures of the time as fully as the Mechanical Hall of any World's Exposition. He wrote the articles on philosophy, sifting into them, so far as the exigencies of the censure would permit, all the radicalism of which he was the exponent, and so realized the great dream of Bacon, to prepare and hasten the future by an inventory of the past.

Of course, he had his collaborators, had his co-editor Dalembert. But it was Diderot, rather than Dalembert, who created the book, rallying the contributors, sticking to his purpose when, seven volumes only completed, a royal interdiction caused the desertion of his fellow-editor, —

Diderot who, through the twenty long years which the work required, "bore upon his shoulders the whole world of the Encyclopedia." In constant danger of police raids, menaced by confiscation and the Bastille, he prepared alone the last ten volumes, remaining in Paris to do so, undismayed by censure as he had been undaunted by imprisonment. In this act of courage Diderot certainly shows all the moral enthusiasm of a reformer. He is a reformer, a *chef de secte*: in the Encyclopedia he founded a lay church for the development of human reason and the perfecting of a new humanity. For this is what the eighteenth century left us, a new ideal for man, man freed from the shackles of tradition and restored to his "natural" rights of life, liberty, and the pursuit of happiness.

All this, of course, sounds very hackneyed today. Yet our forefathers cherished this ideal: Americans, we too owe something to these men and their long-forgotten work. Timid, full of commonplace as it seems to us now, the Encyclopedia is historically one of our great books. It was obliged to proceed by indirection, balancing affirmation by negation, forcing one to read between the lines; but in the long siege against embattled authority and dogma it was the wooden horse of the Greeks. It created history. Making ideas portable, giving the public a primary education in political, social, and economic theory, it prepared the Revolution and the modern world. Asserting the claims of the common people to consideration in the State, it was a pioneer of democracy. A dictionary of the Arts and Trades, it helped to lift manual labor to the category of worthy human achievement. It presaged a new era, and it justly gave its name to its authors, the name of a new sect, fighting for freedom of thought in a despotic age.

Nor was this to be all the service of the Encyclopedia. Aided and reinforced by Diderot's other works, it helped to prepare the literature of democracy. The new popular ideal was already germinating; the day of classicism was over. Objective, intellectualized, created first for a court and always for a public essentially aristocratic, the classical ideal of beauty was destined to be obscured by the demands for a literature more personal and more appealing. After Lesage's comedy-novel, Richardson and Prevost will demonstrate the power of pathos; beside the agile logic of Voltaire, Rousseau will bring out the resources of expression which lie in the sensuous element of style. Literature becomes more human; it stoops to conquer; old forms are expanded, new moulds created, and in this adaptation of an outworn art to a larger audience, no one is more important than Denis Diderot.

Take for instance the question of the drama. He breaks with the old aristocratic conception of the theatre: no more classes, no seclusion of the noble roles in the tragedy — the misfortunes of life do not happen to kings alone. Diderot would put upon the stage not character-types, but conditions of human life; he would create the drama of the people, the tragedy of the middle classes and the serious comedy. Furthermore, he will use the theatre to launch new ideas, to point a moral. "I have always thought," he writes, "that some day they would discuss points of morality on the stage." He put his theory into practice, in *Le Pere de famille* and *Le fils naturel*, and from Beaumarchais to Dumas *fils* and Brieux, from Lessing to Ibsen, we have done little else but follow his example.

Yet judged from present-day standards, Diderot's two dramas are failures. Nothing could be more unreal than their pompous declamatory sentimentality, nothing more evident than their deficiency in objective vision. Diderot lacked the very elements of the *sens du theatre*. He had no deep psychological insight, no taste; and even his dropping of verse for prose, intended as a return to nature, only shows us that certain prose can be more turgid and artificial than the Alexandrine. Nonetheless his two plays, staged in familiar scenery and costumed like the spectators themselves, demonstrated the resources of the new conception of dramatic art. Tears flowed at every performance; women fainted; Beaumarchais, in the parterre, discovered his own vocation for the theatre, and Lessing, witnessing the plays in Germany, wrote his epoch-making *Hamburgische Dramaturgie*.

To move the spectator, to arouse moral enthusiasm, is the end aimed at by Diderot, in his dramas as elsewhere. And as an emotionalist, owing his force to his feelings, nothing is more curious than to find him advocating repression of emotion as the characteristic of the perfect actor. Yet this is what he does in

Le Paradoxe sur le Comédien. Let us interpret the fact, not merely by a tendency to self-contradiction, visible as that is in all of Diderot's work, but as the universality of a mind capable of all points of view, capable ever of criticising itself. For if the penalty of the emotionalist is "to be at the mercy of his diaphragm," Diderot realized it. Forerunner of the romanticists, he voices the keenest criticism of romanticism, and after the suicide of the new school, nearly a century later, his theory of impassibility will find an echo in the naturalists and the Parnassian poets, reaching its supreme expression in the work of Flaubert and Leconte de Lisle.

Self-suppression of any sort, however, we shall hardly find in Denis Diderot. Plebeian, irrepressible, Bohemian, he will show us every side of his garrulous self. Witness his novels, his best claim to fame after the Encyclopedia. *Les bijoux indiscrets* exhibits his taste for the smoking-room story; *Jacques le fataliste*, his determinism and his infinite love of digression. *La religieuse* gives us his ineradicable tendency to moralize; and his disregard of convention and essential Bohemianism are typified in *Le Neveu de Rameau*. Best of his novels, if not of all his works, second only to the Satyricon in its realism, this story certainly betrays Diderot's sympathy for the unscrupulous Rameau, just as his other novels show his sympathy for the garrulous Jacques and the lachrymose Suzanne. So in everything Diderot reveals himself. But he has learned caution by his early experience in the fortress of Vincennes, and prudent as Pan urge, he will print but one of his stories, and that anonymously.

The others were discovered and published after the death of their author. The most original of his novels, they were all but lost to us. For Diderot's stories are original, in spite of all his imitations. He will match Crébillon without Crébilon's wit, Sterne without his lightness and grace, Richardson without his power of delineation, but he is a follower of no one in his genius for dialogue or in the paradoxical brilliance of his thought. For this indeed his novels will be only the vehicle, as in the case of Anatole France. He will never attain the light, whip-like touch of Voltaire, never write a *Candide*; but he will have his own mastery of satire, a satire like Juvenal's; and in *La religieuse*, his realism, pathos, and ethical force will make him not unworthy of his master Richardson. Celebrating the English novelist, moreover, in a characteristic burst of lyricism, and preferring Richardson's concrete reality to the cold aphorisms of Montaigne and the moralists, his comparison suggests the progress of fiction and its new role in literature. An inferior genre in the classical period, the novel of the eighteenth century inherits the realism of the comedy and the moralists, and now, by satisfying popular demands for the pathetic, it becomes a concrete means to a larger audience and a broader appeal.

So at least Diderot, moralist and educator, understood it. A larger audience — he had sought that, as preacher of science against dogma, in the Encyclopedia. A greater public and a broader appeal will be his aim in his drama and in his dramatic criticism. A larger public is what he seeks, as satirist and moralist, in his fiction. A larger appreciation for painting and sculpture will be the intention and effect of his art criticism, the "Salons." A popularizer, he stands opposed to the old aristocratic notion, — the idea that literature and art are for the few.

The "Salons" were accounts of exhibitions, contributed to Grimm's *Correspondance littéraire*. A literary news-letter, this bulletin carried them to all the principal courts of Germany; and just before the end of the century, Naigeon's edition of Diderot made them known to the general public in France.

They popularized art: "Before Diderot," said Mme. Necker, "I had never seen anything in pictures but flat and lifeless colors; it is a new sense that I owe to him." And in fact, a new sense of art as an expression of the human drama came into France through this art criticism. For Diderot believes in the English idea of the picture: he approaches painting and sculpture, like the drama, from the standpoint of expression. As a sentimental moralist, he naturally prefers Greuze, because Greuze delights in pathos and the representation of our common humanity — effects which our critic himself had tried upon the stage. It is literary art criticism that Diderot gives us, but it is undeniable that he imparts the sensation of the masterpiece as well; he relates and explains the subject, attaching himself to its dramatic and moral qualities. And in so doing he practically creates a new literary form.

"A lover of large horizons" — was it Goethe who first called him that? At any rate, Diderot deserves the characterization. "All that surrounds us is a subject for observation," he remarks, "the most familiar objects may become wonderful to us. All depends upon the point of view." The point of view, of course, is only another name for imaginative vision. And Diderot, ever seeking new vistas in drama, literature, and art, finding them, and then relating them to life, did not fail to turn his imaginative observation upon the facts of life itself, to give us glimpses of scientific intuition which justify the nickname given him by his friends, "The Philosopher."

Of course his 'philosophy' is purely realistic. Red-blooded and vital, sensuous and practical, he naturally rejects the abstractions of metaphysics for scientific speculation. Like Comte, he finds the 'how' more interesting than the 'why.' Hence his attitude toward a First Cause which, as a follower of Heraclitus and an antetype of the humanism of our day, he soon abandons as unnecessary. "It is no more difficult to think of the world as eternal than it is to conceive the soul as immortal." His views on this point, however, frequently shifted. "An atheist in town, but not in the country," he really inclines toward pantheism by his feeling for nature.

Let us see now what was his conception of nature. Read the *Entretien entre Dalembert et Diderot*, with its sequel *Le Rêve*. Starting from Leibnitz and his theory of the monad, Diderot goes on to give us the whole programme of transformism, — mineral changing to humus, humus to plant, and plant to man. "The same limestone may become an integral part of the being who possesses the power of feeling, the power of thought." After this conversation, Diderot tells his friend that he will dream of it, and Dalembert does dream, talking in his sleep while his friends listen and comment, and with them building a vision of the world.

It is a world of matter — matter one, but heterogeneous. Even force is not distinct from matter: "The molecule is in itself an active force." Absolute rest, observes this Heraclitean, is an abstract conception which does not exist in nature. Matter contains everything, even the potentiality of feeling; an animal, a plant, is nothing but "an aggregation of molecules united by a bond of continuity." "A swarm of bees, joined by uniting or suppressing their legs" — that is Diderot's idea of the animal organism; and we may compare with it the modern idea of the body as a colony of cells. But Diderot in his search for unity would carry the thought still further; he sees "an indefinite succession of little animals in the moving atom, and the same indefinite series in that other atom which we call the earth." All is one; "every animal is more or less man, every mineral is more or less plant, every plant more or less animal." And death? "The only difference between death and life," Diderot writes to Mlle. Volland, "is that now you live *en masse*; dissolved, scattered into molecules, in twenty years you will live *en detail*." One thinks of the experiments of Dr. Carrel.

But Diderot has not written for the Encyclopedia in vain. Knowing the philosophers from Thales to Locke, his genius catches the opportunities to co-ordinate, to advance upon their work to new ground. Life, to Diderot as to Locke, is "only a series of actions and reactions." But "organs produce needs, and needs, organs," he goes on, and then: "All the faulty combinations of matter have disappeared, and we have left only those whose mechanism contained no serious misadaptation, which were able to subsist and to perpetuate themselves by their own force." Thus Diderot anticipates Darwin, and we are prepared to read his Nietzschean maxim, — "the world is the dwelling-place of the strong."

What becomes of morality in this mechanistic scheme? "A mere instrument endowed with feeling and memory," can man exercise free-will? Evidently not. Will, to Diderot, is the acquiescence of attraction perceived in consciousness; "a man moves on as inevitably to glory or ignominy as a ball which might be conscious of itself follows the slope of a mountain." Every one of our actions has its cause; we cannot know the whole causative series, but we "do only what it is necessary to do." "There are only physical causes, only one sort of necessity; the physical and the moral worlds are one." Moreover, what would be the use of free-will? "The enjoyment of a liberty which could be exercised without motive would be the veritable characteristic of a maniac."

How then shall we define virtue? "Virtue is well-doing"; one is virtuous if he is "fortunately born," and "the criminal is a monster." Virtue is a matter of latitude, as Diderot shows in the *Supplement au voyage de Bougainville*. "We have only to yield to nature's laws," and as we are a part of a mechanistic universe," self-esteem, shame, and remorse are puerilities founded on ignorance and vanity." So, like Anatole France, to whom he has given many a brilliant paradox, Diderot draws from fatalism an infinite indulgence; "not to reproach others for anything, not to repent of anything, these are the first steps toward wisdom."

How little this squares with Diderot's moral enthusiasm ! A fatalist in theory, he abandons determinism in his practice. He is always the moralist, he cannot help moralizing, any more than Rousseau; he moralizes, not because Richardson taught him, but because he is urged to it by the violence of his temperament. Only in the moralist's attitude toward life could Diderot, like Jean Jacques, find full sweep for his emotionality. The great contradiction of human nature, the conflict between the head and the heart, finds in his utter sincerity its full expression; and the fact that his heart rules his head stamps him as a precursor of romanticism.

He is a romanticist, in that we can best interpret his works through his personality. He is a romanticist in the fact that his personality is more interesting than his works. He wins our sympathy by his tremendous human qualities, by his virility and his force, by his very excess. Garat has told us how Diderot took him, a stranger eager to make his acquaintance, into the bosom of his voluble confidence, putting his arm around him, overwhelming him in the torrent of a lyrical monologue which led through a dozen digressions. Catherine of Russia has confessed that she placed a table between the grateful philosopher and her knees, to save them from the fury of his gestures. Extreme in everything, "able to take nothing moderately, either pain or pleasure," delighting in his sensibility, shedding tears on every occasion, carried away by Richardson till he cries "Don't believe him" — like the boy in the melodrama — he has all the defects of our poor humanity. Yet compare him with Voltaire. No balance-wheel of humor controls this Diderot, whose heart, at the autopsy, was found to be two-thirds as large again as those of ordinary men; he gives way instinctively to his temperament, and only once do we note the cry: "I dare not follow myself further, for fear of being absolutely unintelligible." Incessantly enthusiastic, quarrelling with his closest friends when he cannot kindle them to his way of thinking, lacking in the objectivity which alone gives distinction,

Diderot is forced to see himself in everything, to talk of himself on all occasions. He is the bondslave of his egotism, controlled by it as well as by his genius.

Yet he always believed implicitly in himself. He believes in his heart, believes in his passion. "It is only passions and strong passions," he declares, "which can raise the soul to great things. To propose to oneself the ruin of the passions, is the very climax of madness." "If atrocious deeds that dishonor our nature are due to them, it is by them also that we are borne to the marvelous endeavor which elevates it." Hence his opposition to Christianity, with its subjection of the passions, and hence, too, his naturalistic philosophy and ethics. A maker of new values, Diderot is the Nietzsche of the eighteenth century, and like Nietzsche, he knows that "to create new worlds one must have within him a dancing star."

It is this perpetual incandescence which gives to his style its fire, its eloquence, and even its occasional turgidity. According to Diderot, "the animal cry of passion should dictate the fitting phrase." It is this which makes him vulgar and even obscene, because the coarser word is "always the most expressive." From this too springs his love of the dialogue form, as the proper expression of his passionately controversial spirit, which saw all sides of an object, phases subdued to consistency in a purely intellectual or academic type. It is this which makes him inconsistent, because to him reason itself is less admirable if not conducted by passion. "Without the passions no more sublimity, either in morals or in works of art," and one thinks of Diderot's long liaison with Mlle. Volland, commemorated by the correspondence which some consider his masterpiece.

Nothing could be more natural than these letters, which present so complete a portrait of their writer. And after all it is not Diderot's philosophy, not his fiction or his art-criticism, it is the man Diderot who most interests us. The man holds us, as in the portrait of the Louvre, by his originality. He holds us through a personality absolutely laid bare, with all its contradictions, a heart burning with more than human enthusiasm, vital and vitalizing, as if it had caught its heat from Heraclitus' primal fire. Faults and virtues, all of Diderot is revealed in these letters, and we think of him as did his friend Meister, comparing him to Nature as he himself conceived her, "rich, fertile, abounding in germs of every sort, but without any dominating principle, without a master and without a God."

Denis Diderot marks the supreme development of eighteenth century individualism. Hating "that tiresome uniformity which our education, our social conventions, our proprieties have introduced," he looms like a Titan against the background of the times. Like his *Neveu de Rameau*, he is the incarnation of the spirit of iconoclasm. He is the enfant terrible of that talkative, sociable, cafe-loving age; he will test all the bases of tradition with the acid of his logic, until the whole fabric dissolves in the catastrophe of 1793. He is discussion incarnate, and returning from his writings to the picture in the Louvre, the portrait, with all its character, seems less vivid than the man seen through his printed words. Yet Marmontel said that "he who knows Diderot in his writings only, does not know him at all." So musing, we recall Darwin, Nietzsche, all the successors of Diderot, who, thanks to a chance of publication denied to him, have left their names on history of the world's thought. And a sense of wasted force, of the futility of human effort, of the fatality implied in all Titanism, comes over us, beside that portrait in the Louvre, where Vanloo has caught Diderot, prince of improvisers and prodigal of letters, in the very gesture and attitude of inspired speech, lips parted, hand lifted, and eyes aflame.

Lewis Piaget Shanks.

© Éditions DUPLEIX

All rights reserved.

ISBN 979-1092019209

Printed in Great Britain
by Amazon